The
CASE
that
SHOOK
the
EMPIRE

The CASE that SHOOK the EMPIRE

One Man's Fight for the Truth about the
Jallianwala Bagh Massacre

RAGHU PALAT and PUSHPA PALAT

BLOOMSBURY
NEW DELHI · LONDON · OXFORD · NEW YORK · SYDNEY

BLOOMSBURY INDIA
Bloomsbury Publishing India Pvt. Ltd
Second Floor, LSC Building No. 4, DDA Complex, Pocket C – 6 & 7,
Vasant Kunj, New Delhi, 110070

BLOOMSBURY, BLOOMSBURY INDIA and the Diana logo
are trademarks of Bloomsbury Publishing Plc

First published in India 2019
This edition published 2025

Copyright © Raghu Palat and Pushpa Palat, 2019

Raghu Palat and Pushpa Palat have asserted their right under the Indian Copyright
Act to be identified as authors of this work

All rights reserved. No part of this publication may be: i) reproduced or transmitted
in any form, electronic or mechanical, including photocopying, recording or by
means of any information storage or retrieval system without prior permission in
writing from the publishers; or ii) used or reproduced in any way for the training,
development or operation of artificial intelligence (AI) technologies, including
generative AI technologies.

ISBN: PB: 978-93-61314-82-7; eBook: 978-93-89000-29-0
2 4 6 8 10 9 7 5 3 1

Typeset in Bembo Std by Manipal Technologies Limited
Printed and bound in India by Gopsons Papers Pvt. Ltd., Noida

To find out more about our authors and books visit www.bloomsbury.com and sign
up for our newsletters

In worship, we dedicate this book to
the Lord Guruvayurappan,
who has always protected, guided and looked after us
and our family.

We wrote this book in order to introduce our daughters,
Divya and Nikhila, and our granddaughter,
Nivaya, to their familial roots.

CONTENTS

Foreword ix
Preface xiii
Prologue xix

1. An Indian in British India — 1
2. The Land of Plenty — 20
3. Masters of Machination — 28
4. Indians Do Not Matter — 43
5. The Jallianwala Massacre — 60
6. Martial Law — 71
7. Backlash — 88
8. The Trigger — 106
9. The Trial — 114
10. The Verdict — 147
11. Reverberations — 157
12. Grey Skies — 162
13. Thereafter — 165
14. Afterword — 172

Bibliography 176
Acknowledgements 184

FOREWORD

History should be the mirror of time and life in its varied nuances. Sometimes frills and embroidery lace it, but sometimes there are voids, too. The book illumines one such void – an epoch that has been the matrix of the development and growth of constitutional governance and rule of law in India. It deals with one of the greatest Indians of the modern era – Sir Chettur Sankaran Nair.

A few words about this legendary figure's contributions:

There is a little village called Mankara by the Nila River around which lores and legends live, where time stands still even today. Colonel Humberston, who was leading the British army against Tipu Sultan, makes mention of this village and an aristocratic family, Chettur Tarward, into which Sir Chettur Sankaran Nair was born in the year of the Mutiny of 1857. After his early years, he moved to Madras for his higher education. A brilliant man, he soon became a lawyer, a Member of the Legislative Council as well as the President of the Indian National Congress. He was the first Indian Advocate General of the Madras province, a judge in the High Court of Madras and a Member of the Viceroy's Executive Council – a position only second to the Viceroy, and one that had remained beyond the reach of an Indian.

While he was in the Council, the massacre of Jallianwala Bagh, a blot on history, took place. On a Baisakhi Day many patriotic Indians held a meeting in an enclosed space. When General Dyer reached there with a posse of men, he had the exits sealed and commanded his men to open fire. In the ensuing bloodbath, hundreds were killed and wounded. Later, Indians were subjected to many ignominies such as being made to crawl on roads and salute all Englishmen. Chettur Sankaran Nair was agitated by the British Government's highhandedness and he resigned the high office he held in protest, despite the pleas of leaders like Motilal Nehru, Mrs Annie Besant, C.F. Andrews and others, who requested him to remain in the Council and fight the system from within.

His finest hour, however, was yet to come. Nair went to England and carried his mission forward, fighting a case against the powerful Englishman O'Dywer in an English court and, in the course of his defence, convincing the British public – including people like Winston Churchill – about the barbarity of the British Government in India. Consequently, for the first time ever, the Indian freedom movement was discussed in the British Parliament when Ramsay McDonald was prime minister. This was a milestone.

Nair, however, had to pay dearly for his cause, as will be evident to the readers of this book by the end. He was truly the messiah of the freedom movement, not only of India, but also other British colonies. India's constitutional development started with the 1919 Montagu Chelmsford Reforms which he influenced, and later the 1935 Act. His name will be written in letters of gold in the pantheon of history.

Justice Chettur Sankaran Nair
Kerala High Court
August 2019

PREFACE

At the entrance to the library in my grandfather Ramunni Menon Palat's mansion in Karkitamkunnu, in Palakkad District, Kerala, is a life-size portrait of my great-grandfather, Sir Chettur Sankaran Nair, in the regalia of a member of the Viceroy's Executive Council. I had always been impressed by this striking portrait of a commanding, regal personality dressed in a dark blue velvet tailcoat embellished with a gold-embroidered stand collar and cuffs, white breeches, white stockings and black buckled shoes. In one hand, he held a cocked hat decorated with a gold lace loop, while the other rested on the hilt of a sword that swung from his hip.

Growing up, I had heard stories from my grandparents and my father about 'Sir'. They spoke of him with awe and always referred to him as 'Sir'. They seemed inordinately proud of this larger-than-life figure. I knew he had fought a case in England during the British rule, but did not delve deeper into his life at the time. Possibly in the hope of inculcating discipline in me, my grandfather would tell me about how disciplined Sir was in his habits. When he was a High Court judge in Madras, Sir would wake up at 4.30 a.m. every day. After his yoga and exercises, he would have his breakfast and leave for court. In the evenings, he would drive to the beach for a walk and then repair to the Cosmopolitan Club to read the papers. He would return home at around 6.30 p.m., bathe, spend some time reading sacred texts, eat at 8 p.m. and retire for the night.

On the other hand, my father would tell me of the times when Sir would visit the Hill Palace in Thripunithira, the capital of Cochin State, where my father was brought up. My grandmother, Ratnam Amma Palatt, was the older daughter of Sir Rama Varma, then Maharaja of Cochin. My great-grandmother, the Maharani, wanted her oldest grandson brought up at the palace. My father recalled the times when he would go to Sir's room early in the morning and find him doing a headstand, even at the age of 70, in the *shirshasan* yogic pose. Sir would tell him to join in. My father, not being particularly athletic, tried it a few times but failed quite miserably.

This discipline also extended to Sir's punctuality. He would reach the railway station at least an hour before a train arrived. This was despite the fact that the train would have waited for him, on account of his position, in the unlikely event of him turning up late. After all, it was because of him that the Viceroy, Lord Hardinge, ordered a station to be built at Mankara, his village in south Malabar, in 1915.

We would often visit my grandparents at Karkitamkunnu. One day, while rummaging through some papers, I came across a bundle of telegrams from many eminent leaders condoling the passing of 'Sir': the names included Lord Willingdon, Sir John Simon, Mahatma Gandhi, Jawaharlal Nehru, Mohammed Ali Jinnah and many others. This was when it began to dawn on me that my great-grandfather had been a pretty important person.

On Sir's death, my grandfather took his body to his ancestral house in Mankara. The entire village turned up to pay homage to him. This included the *cherumas*, the *thiyyas* and other suppressed classes whose rights Sir had zealously fought for. My grandfather disregarded the traditions and permitted everyone, regardless of caste or class, to enter the house and pay their last respects to a man who had upheld equality for all. After cremating his body on the fifteenth day, my grandfather, Sir's only son, arranged to feed a hundred thousand people and distributed clothes and oil to them as was customary.

Sir's fame continues into the modern day. I recollect our history teacher at school speaking of Sir's minute of dissent against the reforms proposed by Viceroy Lord Chelmsford. Though I had no idea what he was talking about, I felt proud to be his great-grandson. The librarian asked me if I could get him a copy of Sir's book, *Gandhi and Anarchy*, published in 1922. I did, but did not attempt to read it. At the Guruvayur temple, where our family celebrates all important occasions, Sir had donated a bronze *deepastambham* (temple lamp) 24 feet tall in 1908 in the memory of his father. The *deepastambham* is today placed at the east gate of the temple, and continues to be highly regarded.

This book came to fruition after my wife and I went on a holiday to Amritsar in 2017. On our way to the Golden Temple, we passed Jallianwala Bagh. As we had time on our hands, and I am interested in anything historical, we went in. The museum documents the tragedy excellently, with boards, newspaper cuttings and photographs explaining the atrocity that had taken place on 13 April 1919. On our way out, my wife Pushpa excitedly showed me a plaque honouring Nair. It was in gratitude for his role in fighting against the injustice and the massacre at Jallianwala Bagh.

My great-grandfather, Sir C. Sankaran Nair's story had always fascinated me, and after our visit to the Jallianwala Bagh museum, both my wife and I realized that his was a life story that we wanted to share. Initially, it began as an exercise to introduce him to our two daughters, Divya and Nikhila. Here was a man who had played an important role in our country's Independence, a part of their heritage they would certainly take pride in. However, as we put pen to paper and began our research on my great-grandfather we realized that his life made for much more than just a family story and what followed became this book.

Nair, as a member of the Viceroy's council, was an integral part of the British era in India; consequently, that led to us doing a lot of research on the British rule in India, which included the Jallianwala Bagh massacre. It was then that we began to appreciate why Nair had refused to apologize to Sir Michael O'Dwyer. As a member of the British government at the time, he was privy to its workings and knew that, as the Lieutenant Governor, the final decision to attack the innocent protesting in Jallianwala Bagh lay with O'Dwyer. The fact that Nair had been a part of the government that had so brutally butchered his own countrymen must have weighed heavily upon his conscience. To uphold this truth and to expose the Punjab atrocities (of which even he had been kept unaware for some time) he took on this fight alone. Even though the Jallianwala Bagh massacre and the Punjab atrocities were terrible, very few knew of the true extent of the horrors – it was only when this case became famous did these come to the fore, shocking the world.

Our primary sources of research on the Punjab atrocities including the Jallianwala Bagh massacre were the Disorders Inquiry Committee Report (commonly referred to as the Hunter or Hunter Committee Report), The Congress Report on the Punjab Disorders (helmed by Mahatma Gandhi), the autobiography of C. Sankaran Nair and *India As I Knew It* by Sir Michael O'Dwyer, the then Lieutenant Governor of the Punjab, along with *The Life of General Dyer* by Ian Colvin, Punjab Disturbances April 1919 compiled from the Civil and Military Gazette, and *An Indian Diary* by Edwin S. Montagu, Secretary of State for India from 1917–1922.

The case was extensively reported in the newspapers and we were able to source the actual accounts as reported in *The Hindu* between 30 April 1924 and 5 June 1924. In addition to these, we were also able to source news reports of this period from the *Westminster Gazette*, *The Tribune*, *The Forward* and *The Leader*.

In writing this story we have recreated some scenes based on the incidents narrated in our source documents such as the autobiography of Sir C. Sankaran Nair and the books on Nair written by his sons-in-law, K.P.S. Menon and Sir C. Madhavan Nair. In addition to this, we have expanded on and described incidents and situations to bring to life the characters in this story and an era long gone by.

This book was written to inform readers about the atrocities committed in the Punjab by the British, and Sir Nair's instrumental role in bringing them to light around the world, beginning with his resignation from the Viceroy's Executive Council (an unheard-of act by an Indian at the time), and leading to the highly publicized defamation suit filed against Nair by Sir Michael O'Dwyer, who was Lieutenant Governor of the Punjab at the time.

Raghu Palat
Mumbai, 2019

PROLOGUE

The Royal Courts of Justice is surrounded by the four Inns of Court on the Strand, within Westminster and near its border with London. One of the largest courts in Europe, its imposing grey stone edifice in the Gothic revivalist style designed by architect George Edmund Street as a Victorian palace is a marvel. Two iron gates on the front open up to elaborate stone porches that lead into the Great Hall, built in the cathedral nave style. The outer porch has busts of distinguished judges and lawyers who have served in the court. A carving of Jesus Christ stands at the highest point of the arch. On either side at a lower level are statues of King Solomon and Alfred the Great. At the Judges' entrance on the northern front are statues of a cat and a dog, representing the litigants. Its stained glass windows have the coats of arms of Lord Chancellors and Keepers of the Great Seal. A beautiful mosaic marble floor greets the visitors, while its walls and ceilings are extensively panelled in oak and elaborately carved. There are more than 1,000 rooms here, including various meeting chambers, administrative offices, and at least 78 court rooms. Additionally, there are more than 5 kilometres of corridors. The interior is filled with statues and portraits of several famous individuals associated with law and justice, including judges who once administered the law from these courts.

The Royal Courts house the Court of Appeal and the High Court of Justice. The High Court has three divisions – the King's Bench, the Chancery and the Family Division – of which the King's Bench is the most important. The King's Bench is derived from the royal court first established by William the Conqueror in the eleventh century. The royal court, called the *curia regis*, was not a judicial body but an assembly of English lords and nobles that resolved matters of special importance to the king. It was reorganized in the thirteenth century and renamed Court of the King's Bench with professional judges, and remains the highest court of common law in England and Wales.

It was these halls of the King's Bench that heard the case of an Indian who, at the height of English power in India, refused to be intimidated and was prepared to defend himself singlehandedly. On 30 April 1924, the court heard the defamation case filed by Sir Michael O'Dwyer against Sir Chettur Sankaran Nair. While O'Dwyer was the former Lieutenant Governor of Punjab, Nair had been a former Member of the Viceroy's Executive Council, a former President of the Indian National Congress and a former Judge of the Madras High Court. This monumental case lasted five-and-a-half weeks, one of the longest in the history of the King's Bench. The case's proceedings were avidly followed by the Empire, and brought to the fore British atrocities in Punjab. When the horrors were revealed, they convinced the Indians that they needed self-government, as they would never be treated fairly or justly by the British. This case strengthened the nationalist cause in India and gave an impetus to Mahatma Gandhi's agitation. Moreover, the English realized that, to keep the peace, reforms had to be made allowing Indians a say in the administration of India. This ultimately led to the three Round Table Conferences of 1930–32 and the India Independence Act of 1935.

AN INDIAN IN BRITISH INDIA

Govindan, the smartly-dressed white-liveried chauffeur, held the door open for Lady Kathleen Simon, wife of British Cabinet Minister Sir John Simon, to seat herself in his employer, Sir Chettur Sankaran Nair's gleaming black Bentley. This was in late 1929, just after the Simon Commission had concluded its work. Lady Simon was on a visit to southern India and wished to explore the Malabar. As her husband was detained in Delhi, Nair, a good friend of the family, had agreed to escort her – Malabar being his home state. Govindan was inordinately proud of 'his' car and ensured that the Bentley shone to perfection at all times. After all, he was one of the very few who could boast of driving a British car and enjoyed the attention it garnered.

Lady Simon slid into the leather upholstered seat without so much as a glance at Govindan, making sure her flowing white lace dress remained perfectly draped around her, her delicate ankles well hidden from native eyes. Once she had settled in comfortably, Nair entered the car and sat diagonally across from the lady allowing her both space and comfort. After instructing Govindan to drive to the Cannanore cantonment, he slid the glass divider between the chauffeur and passenger sections shut.

As the car sped through empty roads, children smiled and waved while adults tried to get a glimpse of Nair and the *velakaruthy madama* (white lady) sitting in the car with him. Nair, having held important positions both in the judiciary and the government, was a familiar and respected figure here. The Bentley weaved its way into the township of Cannanore. Govindan grudgingly reduced his speed and adeptly stepped on the brake every time a group of schoolchildren crossed the street or a never-ending stream of hawkers carrying overloaded baskets of vegetables, coconuts and fish tried to wend their way alongside the Bentley.

All of a sudden, Lady Simon caught sight of a beautiful and fair-skinned girl walking alongside a dark-complexioned Malayalee man. The two were happily chatting and from their body language one could tell they were a loving couple. To any Malayalee, it was apparent the girl was from the Thiyya community, which is known for their fair skin. The Thiyyas were unfortunately, at that time, considered socially inferior as they were toddy tappers by profession. The British were known to have dalliances with Thiyya girls and some of them had even married British officers. Lady Simon commented, 'There goes a peach of a girl. What could she have found in that ugly black native to marry him?'

Nair was not one to allow such an observation to go unchallenged. He immediately retorted, 'Oh, that's easily explained. The girl has some English blood in her and she is so ashamed of it that she has picked the darkest Indian she could come across so that her children might not suffer from that taint.'[1] Lady Simon, though highly affronted, felt it more prudent to sit the rest of the journey in silence and gaze at the vivid melee of people and colours outside the car's window.

Nair continued to look at the surroundings that were so familiar to him. His father, Manmayil Ramunni Panicker, had been a tehsildar, the highest position available to an Indian at the time, in Cannanore. On his left was the dirt road that led to the school he had attended in this town, and where he had been taught by English teachers for the first time. His love for the English classics, his confidence to question and debate, his deep interest in history and, of course, his command over the English language were imbibed from these teachers. He fondly remembered Cecil M. Barrow, who was especially kind and caring and had inculcated the habit of reading in him. He could see the tiled roof of the school building and the open patch of the playground in the distance. He recalled the robust game he had played with his friends – a much rougher version of kabaddi that is not played anymore. It involved a group of boys in a circle and an equal number outside the circle. One group would try to drag the boys outside the circle, while those inside could push, kick and use any kind of physical force to avoid being dragged out. Fortunately, the teams would swap turns so that everyone ended up equally battered and bruised. He smiled at the memory; the game had made him stronger and tougher.

---

1 Menon, K.P.S., *C. Sankaran Nair: Builders of Modern India*, New Delhi: Publication Division, Ministry of Information and Broadcasting, 1974, p. 135.

They arrived at the cantonment and after showing Lady Simon around the base, he left her to enjoy lunch with some British officers and their wives, and politely excused himself and headed back home. As he sat back comfortably in his car and looked around at the all-too familiar terrain, memories of his early life came tumbling back to him.

Nair had been born in the sleepy village of Mankara, on the banks of the Bharata River, in 1857, the year of India's first war of Independence. Many years later, the Vice Chancellor of Madras University jocularly mentioned while conferring Nair with an honorary L.L.D. that perhaps it was the year of his birth that accounted for his 'mildly rebellious' temperament[2]! The British Government, his colleagues in the Viceroy's Executive Council and his many opponents in the law courts were unlikely to have been as kind when referring to Sankaran's often unrelenting and rigid opinions. Nair was not inclined to be swayed by arguments once he had made up his mind; instead, he would lose his temper when counter-arguments or suggestions were put to him to change his stance. Edwin Montagu, Secretary of State for India, described Nair 'as an impossible person... He shouts at the top of his voice and refuses to listen to anything when one argues, and is absolutely uncompromising.'[3]

During his early years, his parents, M.R. Panicker and Parvathy Amma, were concerned when the boy refused to speak. Their fervent prayers were answered when Nair finally spoke his first words at the age of five. It was ironic

---

2 Menon, K.P.S., *C. Sankaran Nair: Builders of Modern India*, New Delhi: Publication Division, Ministry of Information and Broadcasting, 1974, p. 9.
3 Montagu, Edwin S., *An Indian Diary*, London: William Heinemann Ltd., 1930, p. 31.

that the boy who spoke so late went on to excel in a profession that relied entirely on the art of speech. Yet, all through his life, Nair was afflicted with a speech defect and could never pronounce the letter 'R', though this did not in any way hamper him.

Nair's family members were well versed in kalaripayattu – a martial art – on his father's side and ran *kalaris* (gymnasiums) in the region. Nair, too, like the other children in the family, was trained in arms. It was said that some Nair youth were so proficient at kalaripayattu that they never needed to be burdened with thatched bamboo umbrellas during the torrential Malabar monsoon as they could, with swift and adept flicks of their stick, keep raindrops at bay and remain totally dry. This early training in the martial art, which required great discipline, shaped Nair and he lived an ordered life with strict timings his entire life. It made him a creature of habit; he also expected others to follow his regimen.

In Kerala, Nairs were traditionally soldiers, and Nair thus had great pride in the martial traditions of his community. It was because of this that he did not believe in Mahatma Gandhi's doctrine of non-violence and was emphatic in stating that non-violence was 'not for us Nairs'[4]. Nairs were taught to retaliate when attacked and defend themselves. 'I draw the line when asked to turn the other cheek to my enemy. If someone were to smite me on my cheek, I would chop his head off,' Nair once said.[5] However, he was not a violent

---

4 Menon, K.P.S., *C. Sankaran Nair: Builders of Modern India*, New Delhi: Publication Division, Ministry of Information and Broadcasting, 1974, p. 12.
5 Ibid

man and did not believe in the use of violence to settle issues. Being a lawyer with strong convictions about the equity of law, he held that India should gain self-government through due processes of the law. It was on this basis that he argued and fought in the Viceroy's Executive Council.

Despite coming from a respected and affluent family, Nair was taught early in life that he needed to work hard to achieve his goals. He had examples to emulate. His great-grandfather had been appointed by the East India Company to enforce peace in the Malabar region. His grandfather was the chief officer under the Civilian Divisional Officer. His father and uncle were tehsildars. His parents knew he had to be literate, and the importance of education was instilled in him at an early age. There were few schools at the time, and he had to walk ten miles every day to attend school. When he returned home, he had to bathe in the *kolam* (tank) outside and only after he had washed up would he be served his meal. He was encouraged to study and excel academically, and this dictum stayed with him all through his life. Even when he was 75, Nair was learning Pali so that he could read the teachings of Buddha from the original text.[6]

After finishing school, Sir Nair enrolled at the Presidency College in Madras. In those days, both students and professors were allowed complete freedom of speech within the college. They were encouraged to express their opinions verbally or in writing without any fear of

---

6 Menon, K.P.S., *C. Sankaran Nair: Builders of Modern India*, New Delhi: Publication Division, Ministry of Information and Broadcasting, 1974, pp. 137-8.

repercussions. On the anniversary of America's Declaration of Independence, students were required to write an essay. Nair submitted one that said England must behave in India or else Bombay would become another Boston Harbour. The principal of the school, Edmund Thompson, accepted this arguably seditious statement in good spirit.[7]

At Presidency, students 'associated freely with officials'. Justice Holloway, a Malabar judge who would go on to work at the Madras High Court, interacted frequently with the Malayalee boys at Presidency and encouraged Nair to read the books he had got from London, including William Stubb's *Constitutional History*. This was his first taste of the law, and also marked the beginning of his faith in the sanctity of the legal system. Holloway would take pains to explain the difficult portions and did not object to the arguments his students put forth; in fact, he often encouraged them. In one instance, a young Nair successfully argued with the judge that the Nairs were the only race that had never been conquered by a foreign power.[8] It was these interactions that persuaded him to pursue the study of law.

It was also in Madras that Nair faced discrimination for the first time. Trained in the martial arts, he was keen on joining the artillery corps of Anglo-Indians in Madras under the command of James Spring Branson, the then Advocate General of Madras. He enlisted in the corps along with two of his friends and commenced the required training, but a few days into the training, an order arrived from higher

---

[7] Nair, C. Sankaran, *Autobiography of C. Sankaran Nair*, Chennai: Lady Madhavan Nair, 1966, p. 7.
[8] Ibid.

authorities cancelling the three young men's admission after protests from Anglo-Indians. They attempted to be admitted a couple of times more but were not enrolled.[9]

Nair completed his B.A. with distinction, receiving prizes for History and English. He had an insatiable interest in history and on many occasions his knowledge of the subject was tested by his professors. After graduating, he joined the Law College and passed the B.L. Examination at the top of his class, getting top marks in Hindu Law and in Jurisprudence. Nair had found his calling. Sir Horatio Shephard, who would go on to become Chief Justice at the Madras High Court, took him on as an apprentice, where he proceeded to devour all the cases he could lay his hands on, gaining invaluable experience reading Shephard's cases and even sitting in court as the barrister's junior. Clients started paying him a fee, and he was able to earn his own living and even pay the hefty enrolment fee required to enrol as a *vakil*.[10] He was fortunate that nobody else from his district in Malabar practiced as a *vakil,* and he was offered several cases the very day he enrolled. At this time, there was a clear divide between English barristers and Indian *vakils*. The *vakils* in Madras resented the manner with which they were treated by English barristers, and had passed a resolution that no Indian *vakil* should act as a junior to an English barrister. Even though he had recently enrolled,

---

9   Nair, C. Sankaran, *Autobiography of C. Sankaran Nair*, Chennai: Lady Madhavan Nair, 1966, p. 12, para 18-19.

10   At that time, barristers were usually Englishmen and admitted to one of the Inns of Court in England. *Vakils* were Indians who had passed the Bachelor of Law examination. The barristers tended to be favoured for cases both by clients and judges (largely Englishmen) and had *vakils* as their juniors assisting in research and in preparing briefs.

Nair opposed the resolution on principle; he felt that nothing should be permitted to interfere with the right of a lawyer to choose a senior that his client liked.[11]

Nair's defiance made him unpopular and he was boycotted by the other *vakil*s. But he refused to be slighted. When he became a judge in Madras, it was customary for every new judge to visit the other judges in their chambers and introduce themselves. When an English judge joined the Madras High Court sometime in 1912, the Chief Justice, an Englishman, invited all the judges to his chambers to avoid the new judge having to go to the Indian judges' chambers. Nair, who was with the Chief Justice at the time, went back to his own chamber before the other judges arrived. The new judge was thus not introduced to him, and the Chief Justice's plan was thwarted.[12]

This would become the norm throughout his career. Nair would fight, alone and regardless of others' opinions, for what he believed was right. This held true even when he was in the Viceroy's Executive Council and wrote his minutes of dissent when he did not agree with the Council's recommendations made before the Chelmsford reforms. He was the only dissenting member and did not succumb to pressure from the Viceroy or his colleagues in the Council. He would also fight dispassionately for the downtrodden. After attending the Third National Congress in 1887, Nair threw himself earnestly into the Social Reform Movement. His focus was on eliminating caste distinctions and on

---

11 Menon, K.P.S., *C. Sankaran Nair: Builders of Modern India*, New Delhi: Publication Division, Ministry of Information and Broadcasting, 1974, p. 18.
12 Menon, K.P.S., *C. Sankaran Nair: Builders of Modern India*, New Delhi: Publication Division, Ministry of Information and Broadcasting, 1974, p. 53.

improving the rights of women. Being from the matriarchal Nair community, he had experienced the strength and influence that women wielded in families. Nair women are known to be strong-minded and unafraid of expressing their opinions. This held true for his wife, Lady Sankaran Nair, or Parvathy Amma, too. On their first visit to England, Lady Nair observed that Englishmen carried their children while their wives walked beside their husbands. A few days later, she told her husband in Malayalam so that eavesdroppers would not understand, 'Look here, men are carrying the babies in England, not the women. You too will have to do the same hereafter!'[13] When their son Ramunni moved to England to study at Oxford in 1911, Sir Nair was unable to leave his work engagements to visit him. Lady Nair took the long sea voyage on her own.[14] While she was away, Sir Nair received an invitation from Lord Hardinge for both of them to attend the 1911 Delhi Durbar. In those days, Hindu ladies did not attend government social events. Lord Carmichael, then governor of Madras and a friend, expressed that it would seem impolite if Sir Nair's wife refused the invitation to dine with the King Emperor and Empress. Accordingly, Lady Nair returned in time for the Durbar and attended along with her husband. As she was known to be an orthodox Hindu, other Hindu women too felt it safe to follow her example and attended the Durbar.[15]

---

13 Nair, C. Sankaran, *Autobiography of C. Sankaran Nair*, Chennai: Lady Madhavan Nair, 1966, pp. 43 and 45.
14 Nair, C. Sankaran, *Autobiography of C. Sankaran Nair*, Chennai: Lady Madhavan Nair, 1966, p. 42.
15 Ibid.

Although he was religious, Nair never imposed his beliefs on others. He wrote a book on Christianity where he drew parallels with Hinduism. He read extensively on Jesus Christ, Gautama Buddha and Sankaracharya, figures he most admired. As a Madras High Court judge, his best-known judgment, *Budasna v. Fatima* (1914), was related to Hindu converts, and ruling against such converts being regarded as outcasts.[16] This was radical for its time, as Hindus did not believe one could convert to their religion. In another judgment in 1909, Nair ruled against the prohibition on marriages between Shudra castes, and upheld a marriage between a Hindu and a Christian, which was taboo in those days, in a case he heard in 1914.[17]

Although Nair believed in Queen Victoria's 1858 proclamation of peace, freedom and equality for all the British Empire's subjects, he felt that the British officials in India did not act in accordance with her wishes and treated Indians with prejudice. He sought self-government and dominion status as in Canada and Australia, with Indians governing India. He believed this could be achieved by legislation and it was this belief that made him fight for the rights of India and Indians in the Viceroy's Executive Council and the Secretary of State for India's Council.

In 1897, he was invited to preside over the 13th session of the Indian National Congress at Amroati (now Amravati) – the youngest president in the organization's

---

16 Nair, Sir C. Madhavan, *A Short Life of Sir C. Sankaran Nair: Builders of Modern India, Publication Division*, Ministry of Information and Broadcasting, 1967, p. 40.
17 Menon, K.P.S., *C. Sankaran Nair: Builders of Modern India*, New Delhi: Publication Division, Ministry of Information and Broadcasting, 1974, p. 54.

history till then. In his inaugural speech, he pressed for self-government for India and criticized the manner in which Bal Gangadhar Tilak had been tried and sentenced that year. He brought to attention the fact that the British government could arrest and imprison an Indian without any judicial enquiry whereas an Englishman had to be tried before a jury. He also criticized military expenditure and asserted that 'an army is maintained at our [India's] cost far in excess of what it should be... As England directs foreign policy and as wars are undertaken to maintain English rule, the English treasury ought to pay the entire cost, claiming contribution from India only to the extent of India's interest in the struggle'.[18] He also condemned the thought that the English were superior as a race and kept India in check by the sword in the belief that Indians were not worthy of trust. He insisted on the admission of Indians into public service on an equal footing, noting that all important offices were held by Englishmen.

By the 1920s, Sir Nair had grown to become a formidable presence. He had been a president of the Indian National Congress, a judge at the Madras High Court and a member of the Viceroy's Executive Council. Sir Ramaswami Aiyar, then Congress secretary, had mentioned to Edwin Montagu, Secretary of State for India, that any plan he presented should be approved by Nair as 'he wielded more influence than any other Indian'.[19] He told Montagu that anything

---

18 Menon, K.P.S., *C. Sankaran Nair: Builders of Modern India*, New Delhi: Publication Division, Ministry of Information and Broadcasting, 1974, pp. 39 and 40.

19 Montagu, Edwin S., *An Indian Diary*, London: William Heinemann Ltd., 1930, p. 177.

Nair commended to the Indians, the Indians would accept, but if this was not done, nobody else could make them accept it.

Nair was deeply sensitive to any kind of disrespect, be it from an Indian or an Englishman. He was a proud man, and his pride was often regarded as arrogance. Nair was once invited to be the principal speaker at a public meeting presided over by Lord Pentland, Governor of Madras, to mark the first anniversary of the First World War. When he arrived at Senate house for the meeting, an Anglo-Indian sergeant asked him for his admission card. Sir Nair explained that he did not have an admission card but as he was the principal speaker, he should be allowed to enter. The sergeant brusquely replied that he had orders to not admit anyone without an admission card. Affronted, yet not deigning to argue with the sergeant, Nair returned home. Lord Pentland, knowing Sir Nair to be a stickler for punctuality, was surprised to find him absent even though the meeting was about to commence. On enquiry, he was horrified to discover that Nair had been turned away. Lord Pentland immediately sent his own aide-de-camp (ADC) to his residence with a profuse apology. But Sir Nair coolly informed the ADC that he had started an oil bath and as it would now take him time to get ready, he could not attend the meeting as it would not be correct to keep Lord Pentland waiting. As K.P.S. Menon, former ambassador and Nair's son-in-law, succinctly says about the incident, '*Hamlet* was staged without the Prince of Denmark.'[20]

---

20 Menon, K.P.S., *C. Sankaran Nair: Builders of Modern India*, New Delhi: Publication Division, Ministry of Information and Broadcasting, 1974, p. 55.

In late 1916, soon after he became a member of the Viceroy's Executive Council, Nair was invited to attend the durbar of the Maharaja of Mysore. On arriving at the palace, he was looked after well and attended to by the *Yuvaraja* (heir apparent). On the evening of the durbar, the Diwan informed Nair that it was customary for guests to present the Maharaja with a gold mohur at the durbar. On further enquiry, it was discovered that only Indian invitees were required to make this presentation and not the English. Nair, annoyed at the racial discrimination, said, 'Then I cannot present it either, as I rank higher in precedence than any English guest at the durbar. What would they think if I were to pay homage to the Maharaja? After all, I am not his subject.' He left without attending the durbar.[21] As member of the Viceroy's Council he did rank higher than the average English guest, even higher than the ruling princes. Nair's refusal to defer to authority extended to the British as well. In his book, *An Indian Diary,* Montagu notes that Maharaja Scindia of Gwalior complained to him about Sir Nair not being required to wear a turban while meeting an English official, which the Maharaja was required to wear.

Nair, though a reserved person, would not hesitate to speak his mind in honest and strong terms when it mattered. He frequently found himself rubbing British officials the wrong way and, as a consequence, lost out on career opportunities. When the 1908 reforms were being discussed, he wrote an article in the *Contemporary Review* that made Anglo-Indians furious. In it, he stated

---

21 enon, K.P.S., *C. Sankaran Nair: Builders of Modern India*, New Delhi: Publication Division, Ministry of Information and Broadcasting, 1974, p. 56.

that English juries invariably acquitted any Englishman accused of a crime against an Indian. When Nair's name was considered to fill the post of a judge in the High Court the first time, the Anglo-Indian community petitioned the Viceroy and the Secretary of State for India objecting to his appointment.[22]

It was not just Anglo-Indians who felt threatened by him. When the then Member of the Madras Executive Council passed away in 1911, Lord Carmichael, Governor of Madras, nominated Sir Nair to the council. Brahmins in Madras went on a deputation to the Governor and sent letters to the Viceroy stating he should not be appointed as he was anti-Brahmin.[23] Though once a president of the Congress, Nair took a lukewarm interest initially in the organisation as it was dominated by brahmins and he found his position not agreeable. During Congress meetings in north India, the Brahmins would avoid Nair's company during meals because he was a *sudra* (or a non-Brahmin) in their eyes, whereas in Malabar, Nairs were from the ruling class.[24] He says in his autobiography, 'As we did not want to create a scene, we stayed away from the Congress.'

Despite his relentless agitation for the rights of Indians, he counted British officials such as Lord Carmichael, Sir John Simon and Edwin Montagu as close friends. However, he was not averse to showing his dislike for officials – one

---

22 Nair, C. Sankaran, *Autobiography of C. Sankaran Nair*, Chennai: Lady Madhavan Nair, 1966, p. 38.
23 Nair, C. Sankaran, *Autobiography of C. Sankaran Nair*, Chennai: Lady Madhavan Nair, 1966, p. 43.
24 Menon, K.P.S., *C. Sankaran Nair: Builders of Modern India*, New Delhi: Publication Division, Ministry of Information and Broadcasting, 1974, p. 35.

of whom was Sir Michael O'Dwyer, Lieutenant Governor of the Punjab – especially if they were rude. In 1916, soon after he was appointed as a member of the Viceroy's Council, Nair was invited to tea by O'Dwyer while on an official visit to Lahore. The O'Dwyer's dog, a friendly, gentle animal, approached Nair for a little petting, as most docile dogs usually do. Though he had dogs of his own, he made his displeasure at the intrusion apparent, probably because he disliked his hosts. This led Lady O'Dwyer to comment on Nair's annoyance with her pet. She pointed out that though Indians continually propagated kindness to all living creatures, they did not seem to like dogs half as much as the English did. Nair rudely and rather cruelly replied that this was because, while the English were nearer to dogs in their evolution, Indians had in their 5,000 year history moved further away. British politeness, presumably, prevented the O'Dwyer's from responding to such uncalled for, discourteous and ill-mannered behaviour on part of their guest.[25]

Nair's short temper would easily be agitated by slip-ups and by people who failed to understand his instructions. He tended to shout at the top of his voice when angry. Naturally, most people stayed away from him at those times. He did not believe too much in social niceties either, which was why Sir Lalubhai Shamaldas, a Member of the Executive Council of the Governor of Bombay, asked Sir Edward MacLagan, who had been Nair's secretary and Governor of Punjab, whether he found his manners

---

25 Menon, K.P.S., *C. Sankaran Nair: Builders of Modern India*, New Delhi: Publication Division, Ministry of Information and Broadcasting, 1974, p. 136.

brusque. Though Sir Edward did not comment, his wife Lady MacLagan thundered, 'Brusque! He has no manners at all – good, bad or indifferent.'[26] Even Montagu called him 'frightfully quarrelsome and vilely mannered'.[27] When he was a Member of the Viceroy's Council, he stayed away from the social scene in Delhi and preferred his villa in Simla (now Shimla). This earned him the sobriquet of 'old bear on the hill' and kept his colleagues wondering what he would do next.

His severe criticism of British actions and treatment of Indians drew the watchful eyes of the police even when he was appointed to the Viceroy's Council in 1915. He had on several occasions supported G. Subramania Iyer and Kasturiranga Iyengar, editors of *The Hindu,* when they had written what were perceived to be seditious articles.[28] Once in 1914, Nair invited the Viceroy Lord Hardinge to dinner in Madras, and he asked Congress leader and fellow lawyer Bhupendranath Basu to send some Bengali sweets from Calcutta (now Kolkata) to grace the dinner. Basu sent Nair a telegram informing him that the sweetmeats for the Viceroy would arrive the next night. Unfortunately, 'sweetmeats' was also a code word used by Bengali youth for bombs. The CID, who had been keeping a watchful eye on Nair, intercepted the message and, believing that an attempt was to be made on the Viceroy's life, took possession of the parcel and probably went on to detonate the sweet *chhena*

---

26 Menon, K.P.S., *C. Sankaran Nair: Builders of Modern India*, New Delhi: Publication Division, Ministry of Information and Broadcasting, 1974, p. 129.
27 Montagu, Edwin S., *An Indian Diary*, London: William Heinemann Ltd., 1930,
28 Menon, K.P.S., *C. Sankaran Nair: Builders of Modern India*, New Delhi: Publication Division, Ministry of Information and Broadcasting, 1974, p. 43.

(cottage cheese) dumplings! Thereafter, Basu and Nair were registered as suspects and had the CID shadowing them for the entire duration of the Viceroy's stay in Madras.[29]

Though a devoted husband, Nair did not involve himself with raising his children, which he left entirely to his wife. Diplomat K.P.S. Menon writes in his book, *C. Sankaran Nair*, that he had not come across anyone less family-minded than Sir Nair. 'To his children he was a God, aloof, remote, majestic, a model of all goodness and greatness. Inevitably he left an austere mark on his daughters which even their husbands were unable to efface.'[30] Sir C. Madhavan Nair, another son-in-law who later became a member of the Privy Council too, says, 'He was somewhat reserved and imperturbable in his manners. He was not emotional.'[31] Edwin Montagu also describes Nair's daughters as 'demure, quiet little things' after meeting them at a lunch.[32] This may have been due to them being a little nervous around their father. Though Nair loved his daughters dearly, he did not interact with them at all. His relationship with his only son was also distant. Towards the end of his life, while at Madras, he would have tea with his grandchildren once a week. He enjoyed spending time at the Cosmopolitan Club, reading the papers or conversing with friends. However, he was close to his wife, and her death left a deep void in his life.

---

29 Montagu, Edwin S., *An Indian Diary*, London: William Heinemann Ltd., 1930, p. 70.
30 Menon, K.P.S., *C. Sankaran Nair: Builders of Modern India*, New Delhi: Publication Division, Ministry of Information and Broadcasting, 1974.
31 Nair, Sir C. Madhavan, *A Short Life of Sir C. Sankaran Nair: Builders of Modern India*, Publication Division, Ministry of Information and Broadcasting, 1967, p. 139.
32 Montagu, Edwin S., *An Indian Diary*, London: William Heinemann Ltd., 1930, p. 197.

She had been a kind, gentle lady who had cheerfully taken on all familial responsibilities, leaving her husband free to focus on his work and goals. Their shared interests, too, brought them closer. Apart from travel and reading, they were both deeply interested in the scriptures and would spend some time in the evening going through them with a teacher.

Despite being a member of the Viceroy's Executive Council, the highest office to which Indians could rise at the time, Nair thought nothing of giving up the position and tendering in his resignation in protest after the Jallianwala Bagh massacre. As an advocate for self-government, he fought vigorously and singlehandedly in the Viceroy's Executive Council – not by civil disobedience but by enacting laws. And when he was sued by O'Dwyer for commenting on the atrocities, he decided to take on the might of Britain in the English courts, resulting in a trial that made the entire British Empire, along with the rest of the world, come to grips with the horrors that had occurred.

To recollect the story, however, we must go back a century earlier, to the land of the five rivers, the land of plenty: Punjab.

THE LAND OF PLENTY

Sukerchakia Misl, an independent kingdom in the Punjab, was celebrating the birth of an heir to *misldar* (chieftain) Mahan Singh on 13 November 1780. Sukerchakia Misl was one of the 12 independent Sikh kingdoms that came into existence after the breakup of the Mughal Empire. In addition to the birth of the heir, Ranjit Singh, Sukerchakia had also emerged victorious after capturing the fort of Rohtas and defeating the powerful Chattha chief Pir Mohammed. When Mahan Singh returned victorious, he cradled his newborn in his arms and proudly rode his horse through his capital of Gujranwala to show his people their future chief. Little did he imagine that, one day, the infant would unite the 12 warring *misls* of the Punjab and become the founder of the Sikh Empire.

Ranjit Singh contracted smallpox while still an infant, but the feisty little baby survived the pox, though he was blinded in the left eye and now had a heavily pockmarked face.[1] As a young boy, Ranjit Singh could only read and write in his mother tongue, Gurmukhi. As the son of a Sikh *misldar*, he was trained in horse riding, musketry and other martial arts. Despite his short, stocky stature, he quickly

---

1   Kaur, Madanjit, *The Regime of Maharaja Ranjit Singh*, Unistar Books, 2008, p. 177.

gained proficiency in the military arts. He was an excellent horseman and a fierce fighter. It was not long before young Ranjit began to display extraordinary leadership skills too. He fought his first battle at the age of 10 alongside his father against Sahib Singh Bhangi of Gujarat (a town in Punjab, now in Pakistan) who refused to pay tribute to Mahan Singh.

When the Sukerchakia army marched against him in 1790, Sahib Singh sought refuge in the fort of Sodhran. Mahan Singh laid siege for several months, but he himself fell ill. Concerned that he may die, Mahan Singh called his generals and in their presence smeared Ranjit Singh's forehead with saffron paste, declaring him the next leader of the Sukerchakia Misl. Shortly afterwards, when other Bhangi chieftains found out that the Sukerchakia army was being commanded by a stripling just 10 years old, they marched to the rescue of Sahib Singh Bhangi. Ranjit Singh, however, showed his mettle and mastery of warfare by ambushing and routing the Bhangi army.

Mahan Singh died when Ranjit Singh was 12, and his mother, Raj Kaur, became his guardian. She was assisted by Diwan Lakhpat Rai. Ranjit Singh survived an assassination attempt the next year as Hashmat Khan, the rival chief of an estate, took advantage of an opportunity during a hunt when Ranjit Singh's horse was frightened and attacked Ranjit Singh with a sword. The latter reacted immediately and, before Khan could deliver the killing blow, he cut off his attacker's head.

Ranjit Singh married Mehtab Kaur, the daughter of Sada Kaur from the Kanhaya Misl, at the age of 15.

His mother-in-law helped him consolidate his position. A second marriage to Raj Kaur, daughter of the chief of Nakkai Sardar Rann Singh, made him the most powerful Sikh Chieftain. Ranjit Singh became *misldar* at the age of 18 and began a series of conquests. He began by annexing the other *misl*s and captured Lahore from the Bhangi Misl in 1799 to make it his capital. He then went on to capture the rest of the Punjab. By 1801, he had united all Sikh factions into one state and assumed the title of 'Maharaja' on Baisakhi, the Punjabi New Year, on 12 April that year. He was 20 years old at the time. He continued to expand his territory, and his empire soon encompassed regions from the Khyber Pass in the west to Western Tibet in the east, and from Mithankot in the south to Kashmir in the north.

It has been said that in appearance Ranjit Singh looked like an old mouse with grey whiskers and one eye. He was also short and mean-looking, with a swollen stub for a nose and skinny lips. His head sunk on his broad shoulders that were too wide for his height. His neck was muscular, his limbs were thin and he had small hands. However, when he mounted a horse, his whole demeanour transformed and he assumed a natural grace. Additionally, he was known to be selfish, avaricious, superstitious and untrusting. He was often drunk and revelled in debauchery. His greatness lay in the fact that he was a military genius, a great strategist and a born ruler. 'Men obeyed him with instinct because they had no power to disobey,' writes Griffen Lepel.[2] He married several Sikh, Hindu and Muslim women, fathering

---

2   Lepel, Griffin, *Ranjit Singh*, New Delhi, Shrishti Publishers, July 2018, p. 91..

eight sons but no daughters. However, he acknowledged only his eldest son, Kharak Singh, and his youngest, Duleep Singh, as his biological children.

Punjab during his 40-year rule was stable and prospered. He introduced reforms, modernization and investments into infrastructure. Muslims, Hindus and Sikhs reaffirmed their Punjabi roots and lived peacefully in a truly secular state as Punjabis. Punjabi Muslims, who had for centuries been plundered and massacred by their fellow Muslims from Afghanistan and Persia, were now leading the armies of the Sardar Khalsa against them. Dhyan Singh Dogra, a Hindu from Kashmir, was the Prime Minister. Ranjit Singh called his rule, 'Sarkar Khalsa' and his court 'Darbar Khalsa'. Noblemen from Lahore such as Faqir Azizuddin led foreign affairs, medicine and science departments under the Sarkar Khalsa. New coins called Nanak Shahi were issued in the name of Guru Nanak.

The army was totally separated from administration, as Ranjit Singh put in place an ingenious system under which the army democratically elected five members as 'Panches', who decided on all the matters vis-à-vis the state. Additionally, Ranjit Singh was the first Indian ruler to raise a well-trained, disciplined army, one that was arguably equal if not better than the British army. He engaged deserters from the British army to train his troops. He sent soldiers to Ludhiana to learn English war training and tactics. His Sikh engineers copied cannons presented to Ranjit Singh by the English. After the Napoleonic wars, the French generals Jean-Francois Allard and Jean-Baptiste Ventura joined his services. While Ventura trained and commanded the infantry, Allard was in charge of cavalry. Artillery was under the Punjabi generals Illahi Baksh and Lakina Singh Majithia until the arrival of French general Claude August Court and American colonel Alexander Gardner. The British knew well that his was the only power that could compete with them for the rule of India and were determined to wrest control of the Punjab at the first opportunity.

Unfortunately, Ranjit Singh made some grave mistakes, primarily that he overlooked the need to groom a successor who would ensure that the Sikh Empire remained strong after he was gone. In his latter days, he began to trust and rely on treacherous ministers who worked against him while he remained ignorant of their manipulations.

When Ranjit Singh died in 1839, his eldest son, Kharak Singh, became the Maharaja at the age of 50. As he had had no effective authority or official responsibilities during the reign of his father, Kharak Singh was a profligate. He had no experience or aptitude to rule a nation and was a heavy opium addict. He immersed himself in wine and women. The Dogra brothers – Dhyan, Suchet and Gulab Singh – controlled the administration at the time. Dhyan Singh's son, Hira Singh, had been a favourite of Ranjit Singh's, who had treated him as if he were his own grandson. Dhyan Singh began to plot the death of Ranjit Singh's heirs so that his son could become the Maharaja.

Kharak Singh, however, did not trust the Dogras and started undermining their power. He made Chet Singh Bajwa, his childhood teacher, his mentor. The Dogras were gradually removed from positions of power and they, in turn, retaliated. Chet Singh was ambushed one evening and hacked to death. The Dogras then changed the servants of Kharak Singh and placed him under virtual house arrest. Not content with this, they began to add a slow-acting poison into Kharak Singh's food until he died on 5 November 1840.

Kharak Singh's son, Naunihal Singh, succeeded him in 1840. Naunihal was a valiant warrior and, suspecting mischief from the Dogras, had remained in the North West Frontier where he was the Governor. After Kharak Singh's death, Naunihal returned to Lahore. The funeral procession was underway when he entered the fort. After the cremation, as he and his entourage approached the fort, one of the gates crashed on the new Maharaja. Although Naunihal was not badly hurt in the incident and could walk, Gulab Singh Dogra had him carried into the fort on a palanquin. His mother, his wife and other Sikh nobles were not allowed to see him. Two days later, he was declared dead due to injuries suffered in the accident. It is popularly believed that the Dogras murdered him.

Another son of Ranjit Singh, Sher Singh, was then proclaimed Maharaja. Although popular with the army, Sher Singh was not a shrewd politician but a dissolute who knew more about wine and women than state affairs. He, too, was murdered, and this led to pandemonium, with various nobles aligning themselves with various members of the royal family. Amid this confusing state of affairs, Gulab Singh Dogra ransacked the royal treasury, robbing it of 22 cartloads of gold and jewellery. The loot later helped him purchase Kashmir.

The Khalsa Army and other Sikh noblemen intervened and made Duleep Singh, Ranjeet Singh's youngest, the new Maharaja. Born to Maharani Jindan, the new Maharaja was only five. Hira Singh Dogra, the new prime minister, and his advisor, a Brahmin named Jalla, controlled the administration. He appointed Tej Singh Dogra and Lal Singh Dogra as generals, passing the effective command of the Khalsa army from Sikhs to Hindus. This was done to keep negotiations open with the British if war came, which increasingly seemed inevitable.

At this time, the British were the undisputed political masters of much of India. Through a combination of trade and conquest, their territories had expanded rapidly from Madras all the way up to the Sutlej River – the natural borders of the Sikh kingdom. The British had long had eyes on the fertile lands of the Punjab. In addition, the Sikh kingdom was wealthy and strategically located, bordering Afghanistan and Czarist Russia. While he lived, Ranjit Singh had effectively halted any further British expansion. However, the years of turbulence following his death greatly weakened the Sikh empire.

The British began their preparations to conquer Punjab in 1844. The Ambala and Jalandhar cantonments were tripled in strength with reinforcements and new recruits from Bengal, Awadh and Bihar. Governor General Henry Hardinge began sending more forces to Ferozepur. At the time, the Khalsa army was much larger and stronger than the British forces, and if they had attacked the British at Ferozepur and other cantonments while they were being strengthened, victory was almost certain. The British began to scheme, bribe and played to the egos of Sikh nobles. They promised them great tracts of land and titles if they agreed to betray the new Maharaja when the time was right. One of these was the Sikh Prime Minister Lal Singh, who was in treasonous communication with Captain Peter

Nicholson, the Assistant Political Agent of Ferozepur. Lal Singh hence did nothing for four months, during which the British forces grew to thrice the size of the Khalsa army.

In 1845, at the Battle of Mudki, Lal Singh deserted the Sikh army and ran away. The Khalsa army did not flee, however, and inflicted heavy casualties on the British. The Battle of Ferozepur took place a few days later, and it seemed certain that the Sikhs would win. But at a crucial time, Lal Singh came to the rescue of the British and, lacking leadership, the Sikhs lost the battle. Refusing to accept defeat, the Sikhs retaliated by marching onto Ludhiana and torching the British cantonment. In the battle that followed at Baddowal, Sir Henry Smith was defeated. However, additional reinforcements soon arrived for the British, and the last battle between the British and the Sikhs took place at Sobraon in February 1846. Though betrayed by their own and fighting against overwhelming odds, the Khalsa army led by Sham Singh Attari fought till the bloody end.

In 1849, Lord Dalhousie put an end to the sovereignty of the Sikhs over north-western India. The Regent was pensioned off, while the British assumed the guardianship of the young Maharaja Duleep Singh during his minority. A British Resident was appointed to direct and control the civil and military administration of the state with a council of ministers nominated by the Resident himself. When the British sent off Duleep Singh to England as a ward of Queen Victoria after forcibly making him sign away his kingdom and turned Punjab into a province, a Lieutenant Governor was appointed. Thus, by sheer stealth and cunning, a vibrant nation was reduced to a British Province.

MASTERS OF MACHINATION

After Punjab was annexed, the British strengthened their hold on the land. They built roads and railways to facilitate the movement of troops to the North-West Frontier and for logistical purposes. A new legal system was put in place and the police force was reorganized in the province. They also reorganized the land revenue system. During the reign of Ranjit Singh, the government was entitled to half the produce. Under the British system, land revenue was reduced and cultivators were asked to pay their dues in cash as opposed to kind. This was welcomed by cultivators in the initial years when the harvest was good and the market price was high. More land began to be cultivated. Canals were constructed. The British also introduced the Mahalwari system, under which a village was collectively assessed for land revenue, the proportion payable by a farmer being based upon the land that he owned. The assessment was based on the average collections of the three previous years. Initially the growth in agricultural produce led to prosperity and with it came ostentatious living. Lavish amounts were spent on weddings and festivals. However, the reforms were the death knell of the farmer. The British insisted on revenue that remained the same regardless of the yield. During a good harvest farmers could comfortably pay their taxes, but the monsoons could be unreliable and there was no assurance of a good crop every year. Additionally, if the harvest was good, the increase in produce often resulted in a surplus and this led to a fall in prices.

As was inevitable, soon the farmers began to clamour to pay their tax in kind, which was refused by the British. With little alternative available and to avoid confiscation of land, farmers were forced to borrow from moneylenders to pay taxes. These loans were extortionate. But farmers had no choice but to borrow. It is estimated at this time more than 80 per cent of the farmers were in debt, which was inherited by farmers' children. If loans were not repaid in time, moneylenders could foreclose on the land with the help of the new British laws.[1]

~

The Punjab Land Alienation Act of 1900 was ostensibly passed to protect farmers from moneylenders. The Act created an 'agricultural tribe' to which one had to belong to buy or sell farm land. However, the Act also stated that moneylending castes such as Khatris, Aroras and Banias could not purchase agricultural land. This limitation to transfer of land ownership created huge discontent and did nothing to alleviate rural indebtedness. The 1906 Colonization Bill then allowed for the transfer of property of a person after his death to the government if he had no heirs (similar to Lord Dalhousie's infamous Doctrine of Lapse). The result

---

1   Talbot, Ian A., 'The Punjab Under Colonialism: Order and Transformation in British India', Southampton: University of Southampton, January 2011.

of this legislation was that the British Government could now acquire huge stretches of land in the Punjab at no cost, which they sold to large landowners such as the Tiwanas to buy their loyalty to the Crown.

These partisan legislations fuelled the growth of nationalism in the Punjab. Agitations broke out, and an attempt was even made to assassinate the Viceroy Lord Curzon in 1909. It was during this turbulent period that Lord Morley, Secretary of State for India, appointed Sir Michael O'Dwyer as Lieutenant Governor of Punjab in December 1912.

O'Dwyer was the sixth son of John O'Dwyer, a Catholic Irish landowner farmer who was not particularly wealthy and who, with a family of 14 children, could only provide Michael with an education but certainly could not leave him with an inheritance. The junior O'Dwyer decided to seek his fortune in India. He was successful in the Indian Civil Service examination and after his initial training arrived in Lahore in November 1885. He was first posted as Assistant Commissioner in Shahpur, and then as Political Resident in the North-West Frontier Province. After a short stint as Resident in Hyderabad, he succeeded Sir Louis Dane as the Lieutenant Governor of Punjab.

Fair-haired, blue eyed and stern, O'Dwyer was the quintessential Britisher. Montagu described him as 'a little, rough Irishman with great vigour of expression'.[2] Morley considered him the most illiberal Anglo-Indian statesman

---

2   Montagu, Edwin S., *An Indian Diary*, London: William Heinemann Ltd., 1930, p 32.

that he had seen.³ O'Dwyer enjoyed sports and was an accomplished cricketer. He was a good rider and a keen hunter. He was fond of fencing, shooting and hawking. He was courageous, intelligent and grasped matters quickly, although he was a strict disciplinarian. He had a dislike for politics and a distrust of politicians. And he was a firm believer in the idea that the use of force was the way to get matters settled.⁴

When he was posted as Hyderabad Resident in 1908–09, the Nizam had an English driver who drove recklessly and on one occasion ran over an old woman. The Nizam was distressed and sent a generous gift to the woman's family. However, no action was taken against the driver. As the driver continued to drive outrageously, O'Dwyer took action by calling the driver aside and told him that while he was free to drive as he wished in the Nizam's territory, if there were any complaints regarding speeding in the cantonment and if he killed anyone on British territory (cantonment), he would be hanged. No further complaints were received thereafter.⁵ Philip Mason mentions in his book, *The Men Who Ruled India,* that 'the Lawrence tradition had not died and in the Punjab more than anywhere it was the first article of faith that the man who is most ready to use force at the beginning will use least in the end. The second that juniors must be given a

---

3   Nair, C. Sankaran, *Autobiography of C. Sankaran Nair*, Chennai: Lady Madhavan Nair, 1966, p 350.

4   Mittal, S.C., *Freedom Movement in India 1905–29*, New Delhi, Concept Publishing Company, 1977, p 74.

5   O'Dwyer, Michael, *India As I Knew It*, London: Constable & Co Ltd, 1925, p 91.

free hand and backed with unswerving loyalty.'⁶ Lawrence was the first Lieutenant Governor of the Punjab.

O'Dwyer preferred the zamindar landowners and peasantry to the moneylending and educated class. In his book *India As I Knew It*, he writes that having been raised on the green pastures of Ireland, 'my heart has always gone out to those who live and were raised on the land.'⁷ He believed that the educated class posed a threat to the stability of British rule in India and were the fomenters of rebellion. Like many other Britishers posted in India, he believed that God had ordained Great Britain to govern the world. O'Dwyer believed British authority would be weakened if higher posts were given to Indians and such appointments would encourage lawlessness.⁸ He was intolerant of the growing wave of nationalism in India and believed that India was won by the sword and must forever be preserved by it.⁹

As Lieutenant Governor, O'Dwyer was quite literally a king. He was in charge of the administration of the province and was not answerable to anyone. There was no executive council in Punjab like there was in Bombay, Calcutta and Madras. Though there was a legislative body, he could veto any law passed.

---

6   Mason, Philip, *The Men Who Ruled India*, New Delhi: Rupa Publications, 1992, p 236.
7   O'Dwyer, Michael, *India As I Knew It*, London: Constable & Co Ltd, 1925, p 1.
8   Mittal, S.C., *Freedom Movement in India 1905–29*, New Delhi, Concept Publishing Company, 1977, p 94.
9   Malaviya, Kapil Deva, *Open Rebellion in the Punjab*, Allahabad: Abhyudaya Press, p 7; Ilahi, Shereen Fatima, 'Empire of Violence: Strategies of British Rule in India and Ireland in the Aftermath of the Great War', Austin: University of Texas, 2008, p 35.

When O'Dwyer assumed charge in May 1913, Viceroy Hardinge of Penhurst mentioned to him that there was discontent in the Punjab and as the people were disturbed and upset, he should handle them carefully. However, O'Dwyer chose not to heed his advice. Shortly after assuming office, he announced in a durbar at Rawalpindi and at the Legislative Council that, in his opinion, Indians were not ready for self-government and he would not even consider it. Though he has written in *India As I Knew It* that, as a civil services man, he looked at both sides of the issue of Indian self-government, his words or his actions did not indicate this. He seemed to be blind to growing concerns of Indians and their agitations. In no uncertain terms, he had made his opinions on self-government apparent. 'India would not be fit for self-government much before doomsday (or would she be fit for it even then?).'[10]

In Punjab, he restricted the freedom of the press under the Press Act of 1910. Security was demanded from several vernacular newspapers; the security of a few newspapers was forfeited. His intolerant approach was obvious in his very first speech as President of the local Legislative Council in 1913. On that occasion he warned the press, 'If the action already taken does not have the desired effect, the Government will deal with the offenders as with any other individuals that break the law by promoting disorder or disaffection, and will employ all the means the law places at its disposal, and of these the taking and forfeiture of the security are the least.'[11]

---

10 Nair, C. Sankaran, *Autobiography of C. Sankaran Nair*, Chennai: Lady Madhavan Nair, 1966, p 359

11 Nair, C. Sankaran, *Autobiography of C. Sankaran Nair*, Chennai: Lady Madhavan Nair, 1966, p 350.

It was in this unhappy, discontented atmosphere in the Punjab that the First World War was declared on 4 August 1914 and, in India, the Defence of India Act 1915, also referred to as the Defence of India Regulations Act, was passed. Its intent was to inhibit nationalist and revolutionary activities during the War. The law was enforced during the war and for six months thereafter for public safety and the defence of British India. By this law, it was illegal for anyone to communicate with the enemy, obtain information, spread false reports, or be involved in any activity that the Government, in its wisdom, felt was harmful to the war effort. Like the British Defence of the Realm Act, it gave the Executive extensive powers. This included incarceration without trial, detention and restriction of free speech, of writing and of movement. However, whereas the English law was applicable to only persons of hostile associations or origin (people who were not British), the Defence of India Act could be applied to any subject of the King Emperor, and was primarily used against Indians, especially those suspected of nationalist views. The Act was used to curb freedom of speech, restrict political dialogue and discussion and was a means to jail political leaders.

By June 1917, 705 Indians were under home arrest under the Act, along with 99 imprisonments. Through the war, more than 1,400 people were jailed under the Defence of India Act alone, and a further 300 subjected to minor restrictions, while more than 2,000 were subjected to the restrictions of the India Ordinance. The enactment of the law saw 46 executions and 64 life sentences handed out to revolutionaries in Bengal and Punjab.¹² Several Indian leaders such as Abul Kalam Azad, Bal Gangadhar Tilak and Besant were jailed, interned or deported under the Act.

When the war broke out, the people of Punjab bore the brunt of the Act on account of O'Dwyer, who took it upon himself to recommend to the sedition committee in 1915 that trials should not be held for those arrested as that would be a waste of time.¹³ In addition, he recommended that villages that harboured revolutionaries (nationalists) should be fined and village officers who had helped them should be punished. He prohibited the entry of nationalist leaders such as Tilak and Bipin Chandra Pal into Punjab under the Act. He gagged the vernacular press and prevented nationalist papers edited outside the Punjab such as *New India*, *Amrita Bazar Patrika* and the *Independent* from circulating inside the province. He even prohibited the circulation of pre-censored vernacular papers. As a consequence, it became practically impossible for the people to have a free exchange of independent views, or an airing of their complaints in the public press.

At the onset of the war, the Governor General had placed India's colossal resources and its army of a quarter of a million at the disposal of the King Emperor. However, this was considered inadequate and there were demands for more and more men, especially from the Punjab which had the reputation of having the fiercest and the best fighting men in the country. O'Dwyer wrote, 'The Punjab, with

---

12 Popplewell, Richard J., *Intelligence and Imperial Defence: British Intelligence and the Defence of the Indian Empire 1904–1924*, Frank Cass & Co. Ltd, 1995.

13 O'Dwyer, Michael, *India As I Knew It*, London: Constable & Co Ltd, 1925.,

its hardy and martial rural population of peasant proprietors had, since its inclusion in the Empire, been rightly regarded as the "shield", the "spearhead" and the "sword hand" of India.'[14]

Punjab had, at this time, approximately 4,013,920 men of recruitable age. However, only a small portion of them were available. In the peaceful post-1857 period, the British had constructed a small recruiting pool of about 10,000 recruits a year by keeping away from all the castes except 'the Rajput Dogra of the lower Himalayas, the Punjabi Mohammadan of the north-west, the Sikh of the central districts and the Jat of the south-east', who came to be known as 'martial races'.[15]

Between August 1914 to December 1916, the demand for men from war fields was not very high. In 1917, Army recruiters failed to get recruits from Punjab. O'Dwyer, in order to prove himself and to show his ability to get things done, took up the responsibility of supplying the recruits. 'The necessity of removing every obstacle to the successful prosecution of the war, and to the rally of our manpower to the colours, was the key to the policy which I considered myself bound to pursue during the war.'[16] He created a Recruiting Board with himself as president along with five commissioners of divisions, three principal recruiting military officers and seven Indians (three Hindus, two Mohammedans

---

14 O'Dwyer, Michael, *India As I Knew It*, London: Constable & Co Ltd, 1925, p 140.
15 *Centennial Remembrance Recruiting Terrorism during World War I: A case study*, Y.C.Yadav.
16 O'Dwyer, Michael, *India As I Knew It*, London: Constable & Co Ltd, 1925, p 140.

and two Sikhs). With this committee in place, he recruited 91,499 men in 1917 and 105,876 in 1918.[17] By the end of the war, O'Dwyer proudly proclaimed that Punjab had raised about 360,000 combatants, or more than half of all recruits in the Indian Empire, during the war.[18]

~

In 1920, after the war, the government would admit to the Hunter Committee – constituted by the British Government to inquire into the 'Punjab wrongs' – that 'considerable pressure was employed to secure the result achieved. It would be idle to deny the abuses occurring from time to time.'[19]

It was revealed that village officials were coerced to hold 'durbars' to promote recruitment. Those who assisted in recruitment were rewarded, while those who did not were punished. The names of the former were entered in a white book and the names of the latter in a black book. While those in the white book were given privileges and could be made officials, those in the black book were deemed to be members of criminal tribes and put under police supervision. No government officer was to show any favour to any person in the black book. In addition, all their hereditary titles were forfeited. Not only would they not get any titles during their lifetime, none of their descendants would receive any titles. In his autobiography, Sir Nair

---

17   Yadav, K.C., 'Centennial Remembrance Recruiting Terrorism during World War I', *Mainstream* Vol. LIV No. 35, 30 October 2016.
18   *Congress Report on Punjab Disorders*, p 3.
19   National Archives of India, Political No. 377, 1920, p 116.

writes, 'A form of torture more exquisite can scarcely be conceived.'[20] In addition, the names of villages who had not supplied one per cent or more recruits would be entered in the black book. There were instances where people wished to be incarcerated to prevent their names being entered in the black book.

The committee also recorded that men were captured forcibly and marched off for enlistment. Raids took place at night and men were forcibly seized and removed. Their hands were tied together and they were stripped in the presence of their families and made to bend over thorns when they were whipped.[21] Additionally, women were stripped naked and made to sit on bramble bushes and thorn bushes in the hot sun until their men who had been hiding agreed to be recruited. In some instances, the women were made to sit with bramble between their legs overnight. Old men, too, had inhuman punishment meted out to them – they were made to sit 'bare buttocks' on thorns in order to force their sons to enlist.[22]

Officials were dismissed or suspended from office if they did not comply. Farmers who refused to enlist were not released water to irrigate their fields. In some districts, people were asked to choose between joining the army or facing trial. The police were pressed into forced recruitment. False cases were registered against those who had not met their

---

20 Nair, C. Sankaran, *Autobiography of C. Sankaran Nair*, Chennai: Lady Madhavan Nair, 1966, page 365.
21 Nair, C. Sankaran, *Autobiography of C. Sankaran Nair*, Chennai: Lady Madhavan Nair, 1966, page 366.
22 Yadav, Y.C., *Centennial Remembrance: Recruiting Terrorism during World War 1: A Case Study of Punjab*, New Delhi: USI, 30 October 2016.

quota. Magistrates and judges gave the accused the choice of being jailed or joining the army. An individual could go around this by offering another for recruitment. This led to recruits becoming a product valued at between Rs 500 and Rs 1000. The government also accepted recruits through contractors who purchased them for large amounts of money (often contributed by villagers who wanted to avoid recruitment). To avoid being enlisted, medical certificates were purchased by eligible men and there were even some reported cases of self-inflicted injuries to escape enlistment.[23]

Recruitment became such a passion with the Punjab government that even criminals were included. Two Labour Corps were raised from the jails for service in Mesopotamia in 1916, with 5,500 prisoners, one third of the total average of the jail population, sent overseas. The Jail Department not only fulfilled its undertaking to provide and maintain two complete corps, but even supplied for deficiencies in corps from other provinces.

Such forced recruitment tactics resulted in widespread terror and fear. People abandoned their homes at the mere rumour that a government officer was coming for them. The government then passed a law making it mandatory for all persons of military age and elders of the village to be available to officials in their village. The resulting desperation saw villagers often resorting to killing government officials who had come to recruit them.[24] Nadir Hussain, a tehsildar,

---

23 Ahmed, Syed Ali, *The Darker Side of Recruiting from the Punjab during the Great War*.
24 Yadav, Y.C., *Centennial Remembrance: Recruiting Terrorism during World War 1: A Case Study of Punjab*, New Delhi: USI, 30 October 2016.

was hacked to death in Ghullapur. People revolted against tehsildars in Leihia and Dera Ghazi Khan, with the tehsildars narrowly escaping death.[25] In Jangli, when people refused to enlist, they were arrested. When a group led by a Syed (a person descended from the Prophet) attempted to free them, the police fired at them, resulting in several casualties. Saadat Ali Khan Zaidi, the officiating police superintendent was conferred a medal for his action.[26] Villages such as Mardwal, Thal, Bharkan, Adhi Sargal, Adhikot, Chan, Rangpur, Baghur, Rahdari, Mahmud Shahid and Dravi also refused to enlist.

In the Gujranwala district, a deputy commissioner who did not resort to forced recruitment was replaced by Colonel O'Brien, who toed the government's line. The result, in the words of O'Dwyer, was that while 'a year ago Gujranwala had 3,338 men in the Army or only one man in every 150...at the end of the last month, it had 11,756 men in the army which gives a ratio of one in every 14.' How was this achieved? A person from the village Ratali was recorded in the Congress Report as saying, 'The Tehsildar Fateh Khan came to our village... As it was harvest time, and as the people were afraid of being forcibly taken as recruits, only a small number of people attended in the morning. The Tehsildar, therefore, fined some 60 or 70 persons... The people were again ordered to present themselves at

---

[25] *Congress Report on Punjab Disorders*, p 19; Yadav, K.C., *Donning the Khaki: Recruitment in the Punjab during the First World War*, New Delhi: United Services Institution of India

[26] *Congress Report on Punjab Disorders*, p 19; Yadav, K.C., *Donning the Khaki: Recruitment in the Punjab during the First World War*, New Delhi: United Services Institution of India.

Gujranwala, which is 8 miles off. When the people went there on the fixed date, they were made to stand in a row and seven young men were picked out. The other people were abused and beaten.'[27]

The situation was similar in Multan. At the end of December 1917, the district's contribution stood at 759 men – one in 586. By the end of November 1918, the numbers had risen to 4,636 or one in 93. In Lyallpur, lambardars (members of zamindari families who collected revenues) were told if they did not present recruits, they would lose their *lambardari* rights. Magistrates refused to grant bail to those arrested unless a recruit was provided. In many cases, people were not criminally prosecuted if they offered themselves as recruits.[28]

The Punjab government had also compelled Indians to make large contributions to the war funds, with a circular stating that Indians should invest between a quarter and a half of their income in war loans. It was also made clear to wealthy citizens that failure to contribute to the fund would be taken into account during nominations to municipal and notified area committees and during appointments of honorary magistrates and in any other forms of government recognition on the grounds that such honours were reserved for those who had shown their desire to assist the administration.

The Congress Report on the Punjab disorders mentions that judicial processes were also pressed into service for

---

[27] Yadav, Y.C., *Centennial Remembrance: Recruiting Terrorism during World War 1: A Case Study of Punjab*, New Delhi: USI, 30 October 2016.

[28] Yadav, Y.C., *Centennial Remembrance: Recruiting Terrorism during World War 1: A Case Study of Punjab*, New Delhi: USI, 30 October 2016.

raising funds. For instance, the First Class Magistrate at Chakwal discharged an accused in a criminal case noting that 'the accused and his brother have between them subscribed Rs 110 towards "Our Day Fund" and according to verbal compromise made, the accused is accordingly acquitted.' In another instance, the magistrate dismissed the application of a remission of income tax by remarking, 'Owing to the War, the profit of the mules is immense, but the objector has not contributed a pice to any War Fund or any War Loan. He has also a son whom he would not enlist.'[29] Sardar Sant Singh, the then vakil of Lyallpur, has written that 'war loans were forcibly levied in this district. Title-hunters exacted war loan from the masses in order to win honour for themselves. Rs 33 per square-holder was forcibly levied en masse. No exception was made. Even an adjudged bankrupt had to pay it.'[30]

In short, to fulfil their quota and be perceived as loyal and effective, the Punjab government forced an unwilling populace to join the army or to raise funds for the war by cruelty, torture, extortion and threats. A pertinent question now emerges: Who was responsible for these extreme measures? It has to be the person at the helm – Lieutenant Governor Sir Michael O'Dwyer, who ruled Punjab with an iron whip. He had publicly boasted that he would not only meet but exceed the expectations of the King Emperor and, eventually, his inhumane and cruel methods resulted in seething discontent that set the stage for the growth of nationalism in the Punjab.

---

29 Pathak, Rashmi, *Punjab through the Ages,* New Delhi: Sarup & Sons, 2007, p 8.
30 *Congress Report on Punjab Disorders,* p 24.

INDIANS DO NOT MATTER

During the first World War, Sankaran Nair was a member of the Viceroy's Executive Council. He was inducted in 1915 by Lord Hardinge to be in charge of education, health and lands. Shortly afterwards, the Viceroy told Nair he should provide the government with an Indian perspective. Hardinge would send him his speeches to approve, and if they brought Hardinge any trouble with the Indians, the Viceroy would hold Nair responsible. Conversely, if Hardinge disregarded his advice, the responsibility would be Hardinge's own.[1]

Lord Chelmsford succeeded Hardinge six months after Nair was appointed to the Executive Council. Nair's relationship with Lord Chelmsford was not as cordial as it had been with Hardinge. 'From the very first [day], Lord Chelmsford's treatment of me was cold and distant. It was in striking contrast to that of Lord Hardinge.'[2] Chelmsford did not wish to know the opinions of Indians and when these were conveyed to him, he would be visibly annoyed.

---

[1] Nair, Sir C. Madhavan, *A Short Life of Sir C. Sankaran Nair: Builders of Modern India, Publication Division*, Ministry of Information and Broadcasting, 1967, p 63; Montagu, Edwin S., *An Indian Diary*, London: William Heinemann Ltd., 1930, p 143.

[2] Nair, C. Sankaran, *Autobiography of C. Sankaran Nair*, Chennai: Lady Madhavan Nair, 1966, p 83.

One of these instances took place during the discussions that took place post the war. As India had helped Britain greatly during the war effort, providing with both men and money, there was much appreciation for India in Britain and a feeling that a significant gesture should be made to show Britain's gratitude. The Secretary of State for India, Austen Chamberlain, had asked Hardinge to prepare a liberal memorandum just as he was leaving India in 1916. Hardinge's memo suggested the involvement of greater number of Indians while passing laws. Morever, with respect to provincial legislative councils, he wanted an elected majority composed of representatives of constituencies in which the majority were Indians as opposed to nominated members.

However, Lord Chelmsford believed that self-government for Indians should be implemented gradually and be based on growth in education, lessening of racial and religious differences, and Indians getting more political experience. Sir Nair felt the proposals were inadequate and wrote a dissent note that was highly resented by Lord Chelmsford and other members of the Council. The Viceroy asked a British member to request Nair to withdraw the dissent note or agree to not attach it to the dispatch being sent to London. This member would meet Nair every morning begging him, protesting and even threatening him to withdraw his note. He even asked for permission to draft a minute of dissent on Sir Nair's behalf. When Nair did not agree, another member wrote him a letter threatening that the Government could withdraw some of the concessions granted in the report, such as the appointment of Indians to the Provincial Executive Council. Other members, too, wrote to Nair, stating that his minute of dissent was destructive, even suggesting that it corroborated with the German view that India was seething with discontent.

Nair did not budge. On account of the Viceroy's stance and that of the other members of the Council, he asked Bhupendranath Basu, a former Congress president then staying with him, that he and other Indian leaders should state their views. Basu and Sir B.N. Sarma (later a member of the Viceroy's Executive Council) wrote a memorandum. Along with Mohammed Ali Jinnah of the Muslim League (who approved the memo) they took it to other members of the Indian Council.

The 1917 memo, which came to be known as the '19 Members Memorandum', was submitted to the Government of India but the Government refused to forward it to the Secretary of State. However, once it was reported in the papers, Austin Chamberlain, the then Secretary of State, asked for it. Along with Sir Nair's dissent, Chamberlain rejected the government's proposals while agreeing with Sir Nair and said that the time had come to take Indian public opinion into consideration. He wrote to Lord Chelmsford: 'Does your government sufficiently realise that the time has gone by when it was sufficient for it to do the right thing, and that now you must not only do right but persuade people that it is right? You must take into account public opinion. It is no longer possible to wrap yourselves in your own virtues and damn the consequences... Whenever Indian opinion is stirred…the departments explain, "Say nothing!

Do nothing! Pray Heaven, if we are quiet, the storm will pass over our heads. If we pretend there is nothing going on that calls for action or explanation, all will be well"...I am sure this will not do. I am sure this will lead to a bitter estrangement between the government and the governed, that unless you act in time you will someday wake up to find that between you and them an impassable gulf is fixed which it will then be impossible to bridge.'[3]

Chamberlain resigned soon after and was replaced by Edwin Montagu, the son of a millionaire Jewish banker who was a favourite of Prime Minister Asquith. He had a large head and a pockmarked face, and was imaginative, ambitious, devoted and generous. He was charged with exploring the possibility of a remedy for the growing nationalist movement in India. On being appointed, he stated in the House of Commons that unless reforms were introduced, Britain would lose its right to control its Indian Empire. Shortly after his appointment on 20 August 1917, he said, 'The policy of His Majesty's Government is that of increasing association of Indians in every branch of administration and the gradual development of self-governing institutions with a view to the progressive realization of responsible government in India under the aegis of the British Crown.'[4]

Montagu followed this up by visiting India in late 1917 to assess for himself what the Indians were feeling. He met Lord Chelmsford for the first time and commented,

---

[3] Menon, K.P.S., *C. Sankaran Nair: Builders of Modern India*, New Delhi: Publication Division, Ministry of Information and Broadcasting, 1974, p 77.
[4] Menon, K.P.S., *C. Sankaran Nair: Builders of Modern India*, New Delhi: Publication Division, Ministry of Information and Broadcasting, 1974, p 79.

'He has not the dignity of Hardinge or the pomposity of Curzon, but he is quite good to look at, with a fine athletic figure, square shoulders, small hips, well-shaped head and a graceful forward inclination of the body. Conversation showed that he is really a good fellow, thoroughly nice, but unfortunately cold, aloof, reserved. He seems to me to be strongly prejudiced in his views, holding them very, very keenly but I do not seem to see that any of them are his views. They always seem to be collected from his surroundings.' Montagu went on to write that Britain tended to choose the wrong type of persons as viceroys – people who approached problems from the wrong side; who would do what they were told to do such as plough through files and ensure regulations were followed; and who, from a social point of view, were obsessed with precedence and who had no political instinct.[5]

Montagu and his advisers toured the country meeting provincial governors, Indian princes and politicians. He did not get on with Nair at first; unlike others, Nair could be straightforward and had no compunction in arguing loudly if he did not agree with a proposal. Montagu was often at a loggerheads with Nair with respect to proposed reforms. However, Congress secretary Ramaswami Aiyer advised Montagu that it was essential that he should get Nair's support as he wielded more influence than any other Indian at the time.

When the reforms were finally introduced as the Government of India Act 1919, signed on 15 March

---

5   Montagu, Edwin S., *An Indian Diary*, London: William Heinemann Ltd., 1930, p 16..

1919, they were the result of the recommendations in the Montagu-Chelmsford proposals based on the former's visit to India. The new Act provided not for self-government as it was hoped for but for the induction of more Indians into the administration. Though several Indian leaders accepted this as a step forward, Sir Nair believed more authority must be given to Indians in every sphere of government.

India was in a bad shape economically after the First World War. There was a huge shortage of essentials across the country. The price of wheat rose by 47 per cent; sugar by 68 per cent; cotton by 300 per cent and food grains by 100 per cent. Wages were stagnant, but taxes rose between 1918–19 by 30 per cent in Lahore and 55 per cent in Amritsar.[6] As there was very little trade during the war, poverty had increased significantly. The cost of the war was enormous, both in terms of money and in the number of people affected. India had contributed £146 million to Great Britain for the war, and half a million people, of which 400,000 were from the Punjab.[7] It is estimated that around 74,000 Indian soldiers had died in the war, while many more were wounded and maimed.

The suffering endured during the war gave more fuel to post-war nationalist feelings. The moderates and extremists now came together to revive the call for nationalism. The Congress even entered into an alliance with the All India

---

[6] Elllahi, Shereen Fatima, *Empire of Violence - Strategies of British Rule in India and Ireland in the Aftermath of the Great War, Austin*, USA: University of Texas at Austin, 2008, pp 35-36.

[7] Elllahi, Shereen Fatima, *Empire of Violence - Strategies of British Rule in India and Ireland in the Aftermath of the Great War, Austin*, USA: University of Texas at Austin, 2008, p 1.

Muslim League. The feeling of nationalism only grew with the introduction of the Rowlatt Act in February 1919. Known as the Black Bill, it was an extension of the emergency powers the Government had held during the war to control public unrest. Instead of lifting the severe provisions of the Defence of India Act, the Black Bill continued many of its harsh terms such as incarceration without trial and restrictions on the freedom of speech, assembly and civil rights.

The Act had been passed on the recommendation of the Sedition Committee headed by Sidney Rowlatt which had been constituted to determine whether militant groups in India had links with Bolshevik Russia or Germany. Sir Nair, who was consulted for his opinion by leaders such as Madan Mohan Malaviya and Jinnah, opposed the bill. Even though the government was aware of the opposition to the bill, it was rushed through the Council. It was introduced on 6 February 1919, referred to the select committee on the same day, presented to the Council on 1 March, and passed on 18 March by the official majority. Sir Nair was the only member who voted against the bill.

Under the Act, a provincial government, on a notification by the Governor General, could ask a man to notify his residence or change of residence to any specified authority or be instructed to remain in any specified area in British India. Consequently, he might be directed to a location away from his business, which could utterly ruin his livelihood. He was not entitled to a hearing at any judicial court for exemption or claim compensation. He could be required to refrain from doing anything that could obstruct the peace or was prejudicial to public safety. Such orders were not passed after any judicial enquiry and could be passed without even giving anyone a chance to be heard. An individual could be asked to report himself to the police. The government could also arrest any person who they thought had committed an offence without a warrant; they could fine him and search his house. In short, the executive was substituted for the judiciary as far as security of property and safety of persons were concerned.[8]

The executive was empowered to state that certain offences should be tried by a specially constituted tribunal but without any jury or any commitment by a magistrate, and in such locality as the Government might decide, where no competent lawyers may be available. The accused was not entitled to be represented by counsel. The accused was even denied the right to know their accusers and the evidence against them. The accused could, therefore, not prepare their defence, nor were they entitled to give any evidence before the court. Those convicted were required to deposit securities upon release, and were prohibited from taking part in any political, educational or religious activities. The trial could be *in camera*. There was no right of appeal. An investigating authority could be constituted in some cases but the accused was not permitted to be present while their case was being heard. The enquiry was held *in camera* and the government was not bound to accept its findings. Additionally, the act effectively authorized the government to imprison any person suspected of terrorism for up to two

---

[8] Menon, K.P.S., *C. Sankaran Nair: Builders of Modern India*, New Delhi: Publication Division, Ministry of Information and Broadcasting, 1974, p 99.

years without a trial, and gave the authorities power to deal with all revolutionary activities. It also provided for stricter control of the press.[9]

The Rowlatt Act was seen as the antithesis of the fair-mindedness Britain prided itself on. It took away the safeguards one would expect – the right to be defended by a lawyer of one's choice, trial by a jury of one's peers (as enshrined in the Magna Carta), judgment in open court and the right to appeal. It was also seen as a betrayal. The enforcement of the Act resulted in a surge of nationalism. Smouldering discontent exploded in a wave of rage and antagonism. Indian leaders such as Mahatma Gandhi called for passive resistance to the Act, while leaders argued it was unjust and unfair to enact such legislation.

Back in Punjab, the atmosphere was tense. It had suffered greatly in the war due to the loss of manpower, forced recruitment and export of its agricultural produce to feed soldiers. Additionally, the educated classes were frustrated on account of O'Dwyer's attitude, his insensitive speeches and his severe and harsh actions. When the Rowlatt Act was passed, agitations began across the province led by Dr Satya Pal and Dr Saifuddin Kitchlew from the Congress. Dr Satya Pal had served as a lieutenant with the Royal Army Medical Corps in the World War. He was from a middle class Hindu family and was deeply patriotic. He had gained popularity for having carried out a successful agitation against the stoppage of platform tickets issued to Indians at the Amritsar railway station.[10] On the other hand,

---

9 Ibid
10 *Congress Report on Punjab Disorders*, p 48.

Dr Saifuddin Kitchlew had graduated from Munster University in Germany and had a large law practice in Amritsar.[11]

On 29 March 1919, thousands gathered in Amritsar to protest against the provisions of the Act and asked the Secretary of State to veto it. As Mahatma Gandhi and other leaders realized that constitutional procedures would not be sufficient, a strike had been organized for the next day in Delhi. Indians were asked to shut their shops and businesses and fast to show their opposition. But the Rowlatt Satyagraha (as it came to be known) was eclipsed by rioting in the Punjab. Gandhi, feeling that riots went against the principles of non-violence, suspended the resistance. But Punjab continued to simmer. Lahore had been completely shut down that day and, on 6 April, the whole of Punjab went on a strike. The Congress Report reads, 'It was a scene unparalleled in the Punjab, and for that matter, in India. On that day, the leaders and the people seemed to act as one. There was complete fraternization between Hindus and Muslims. Resolutions were passed all over, protesting against the Rowlatt Act and demanding its repeal. The demonstration of the 6 April was a peaceful assertion of the people's will.'[12]

O'Dwyer declared that the strike was illegal (even though it was peaceful) and a conspiracy. The *satyagraha* was also considered illegal. Additionally, on 3 April, he had issued orders that Dr Kitchlew and Dr Satya Pal were

---

11 *Congress Report on Punjab Disorders*, p 49-50.
12 *Congress Report on Punjab Disorders*, p 46.

to remain within the municipal limits of Amritsar and refrain from convening, attending or addressing in person or in writing any public meeting. On 7 April, he told the Legislative Council that a section of agitators who had stayed in the background during the war when loyal citizens were helping to fight a common enemy were now coming forth to show their valour by attacking the government and endeavouring to intimidate and coerce law-abiding people by spreading their propaganda of passive resistance. 'The Government of this province (Punjab) is and will remain determined that public order, which was maintained so successfully during the time of war, shall not be disturbed in time of peace. Action has therefore been taken...against certain individuals at Lahore and Amritsar who, whatever their motives, were endeavouring to arouse feeling against the Government.'[13]

In response, O'Dwyer halted the circulation of newspapers in Punjab. The situation deteriorated rapidly, with rail, telegraph and communication systems being disrupted. At the end of the first week in April, large crowds agitated in Amritsar, Lahore and other towns even as all strikes and processions were prohibited.

Ram Navami that year fell on 9 April. Nationalist leaders had decided that Hindus and Muslims should jointly participate in a rally in a show of solidarity. This was unprecedented. As a long procession of both Hindus and Muslims went around the city, Dr Kitchlew and Dr Satya Pal both witnessed the procession from different places

---

13 Nair, C. Sankaran, *Autobiography of C. Sankaran Nair*, Chennai: Lady Madhavan Nair, 1966, p 376.

and received great ovations as it went past them. Miles Irving, Deputy Commissioner of Amritsar, also watched the procession, and as the various band parties passed him, they struck up the British national anthem, 'God Save the King'. Despite the large numbers, there were no instances of violence.

Dr Satyapal had invited Mahatma Gandhi to visit Amritsar to explain the doctrine of Satyagraha. Seeing the growing unrest, Gandhi decided to accept. However, his entry into the Punjab was stopped at the first station inside the Punjab and he was arrested and sent back to Bombay where he was interned. On 10 April when news of his arrest spread, a procession of 400 unarmed men marched up the Mall in Lahore towards the Government House to plead for Gandhi's release. A few soldiers met them on the way at the O'Dwyer Soldiers Club and told them to turn around. They did not. This resulted in the soldiers firing at them and killing a few protestors. The crowd then retreated to the Lahori Gate. An Indian leader named Rambhuj Dutt Chowdhari, on hearing about the march, arrived and begged the police to permit him to talk to the crowd. The Superintendent of Police gave him two minutes. Chowdhari pleaded for more time but was refused. After the two minutes had elapsed, a few turned back but the police fired again and more people were killed.

The growing national consciousness angered O'Dwyer. He issued orders for the arrest of Dr Kitchlew and Dr Pal. The two were moved to a secret location and from there to Dharamsala.

When locals came to know of the arrest, nearly 50,000 people came together and proceeded to the Deputy Commissioner's bungalow to plead for their release. They were, however, stopped at the railway carriage overbridge leading to Irving's residence. The bridge was guarded by a military picket ordered by Irving. The procession asked for permission to submit a *faryad* (complaint) to the Deputy Commissioner. However, due to the rush of the crowd, the military picket was pushed back. Two from the crowd – Salaria and Maqbool Mahmood, a pleader in the high court – asked the protestors to stop but some of them began to throw stones at the soldiers, who immediately fired into the crowd, killing 20 and wounding many more.[14]

The firing changed the disposition of what had been a peaceful procession until then. The crowd quickly turned into an angry mob seeking vengeance for the wounding and killing of its brethren. The procession carried the killed and the wounded into the bazaar, where the sight of the wounded persons and dead bodies inflamed others. Within a short time, a large crowd had once again gathered near the carriage overbridge, only this time it had armed itself with sticks and logs.

Although some attempts had been made to soothe the crowd after the shooting, they didn't help. The officer in-charge expressed his regrets and some efforts were made to get help for those wounded. Stretchers were brought from the hospital but the Deputy Superintendent of Police Plomer sent them away saying the people should make their own arrangements. An English doctor named Mrs

---

14   *Congress Report on Punjab Disorders*, p 51–52.

Easton had a narrow escape after commenting that Hindus and Muslims had got their just desserts after the shooting. The crowd wanted to drag her out of the hospital, but the hospital staff hid her in a wardrobe.

The crowd continued to show its anger. Several banks, the Town Hall, the railway station and other buildings were set on fire. Three English bankers, two other Britishers, and several governmental employees and civilians were killed. The mob destroyed railway tracks and cut down telephone lines.

O'Dwyer sent A.J.W. Kitchin, the Lahore Commissioner, to investigate. Around 11 p.m. that night, a troop train commanded by Major MacDonald arrived. Kitchin told him that civil authorities could not handle the situation any longer and that the military should take control. When locals wanted to conduct the last rites of the dead on the morning of the 11th, military authorities did not allow more than four persons to accompany each bier. The locals, who wanted a funeral procession, were dissatisfied and sent their representatives to plead with the authorities. Permission was granted, but the funeral procession was ordered to return before 2 p.m.[15]

Kitchin returned to Lahore that day, while Irving handed control of Amritsar to the military on the approval of O'Dwyer. That same day, Miss Marcella Sherwood, an English missionary who was in charge of several mission schools, was on her way to shut the schools and send approximately 600 Indian children home after fearing for their safety. While cycling through a narrow street called

---

15 *Congress Report on Punjab Disorders*, p 56.

Kucha Kurrichhan, she was caught by a mob, pulled to the ground by her hair, stripped naked, beaten, kicked, and left for dead. Some locals, including the father of one of her pupils, rescued her and hid her from the mob, before smuggling her to the safety of Gobindgarh Fort nearby. O'Dwyer then contacted Divisional Commander Sir William Beynon to take steps to restore law and order. General Beynon sent Lieutenant Colonel Morgan of the 124 Baluch to Amritsar as Major MacDonald had failed to maintain order. Just as Morgan arrived in Amritsar, another senior officer by the name of Brigadier General Dyer, who was General Officer Commanding, the Jullunder Brigade, reported for duty. He was accompanied by his Brigade Major Captain Briggs and Captain Southey. Dyer stated that he had been ordered by telegram to go to Amritsar by General Beynon. Since he outranked Morgan, the charge of the city was handed over to Dyer.

Dyer was born in Murree in Punjab to a wealthy brewer and was educated in Murree and in Simla. After graduating from the Royal Military Academy at Sandhurst, he served in the Queen's Royal Regiment and, in 1887, joined the British Indian Army, where he was initially posted in Bengal and then in the Punjab. As a soldier he was, according to Major General Sir Gerald Kitson who had commanded the Jubbalore Brigade that Dyer was attached to, an excellent staff officer having been trained through the Staff College.[16] He was a good rider, an excellent shot and a boxer. Unfortunately, he had a stutter he had inherited

---

16 Colvin, Ian, *The Life of General Dyer*, London: William Blackwood & Sons Ltd., 1929, p 60-61.

from his mother, which gave him a complex. Dyer was an introvert who was shy and extremely sensitive to criticism. He got upset if made fun of and did not have the capacity to ignore any threats. He was a bit of an outsider in the ranks and did not make friends or companions easily. He was also short-tempered and would resort to violence at the smallest instigation. He often unleashed his anger at his subordinates. This made him something of a bully, though he was often known to treat his subordinates with consideration. In addition, he had a tendency to brag to prop up his own self-esteem. Ambitious, he often acted without thinking of the consequences. Although he presented an image of an honest, simple soldier, he listened to no one and took no one's advice. Furthermore, he despised those who thought differently from him. He was not well-liked by his superiors and had often been passed over for promotion. Additionally, he was a strict disciplinarian and a ruthless officer who had little regard for political advice as well as a strong proponent of the power of the gun. He believed his orders in the Punjab were to get the country under British governmental control. He felt that, rather than restore order in the Punjab, it was of paramount importance that the Indians be taught who was in charge. He thought that this rise of the nationalism would result in a mutiny similar to the one in 1857. Therefore, Dyer's initial move when he was brought in to deal with the situation was to arrest 12 local political leaders.

Amritsar was quiet for the next few days, though unrest and violence did not abate in other parts of Punjab. O'Dwyer contacted the Viceroy and advised him that severe action must be taken as a revolt was brewing. Believing O'Dwyer, Lord Chelmsford indicated that he would support any action taken by him.

On the evening of 12 April, the leaders of the strike in Amritsar held a meeting at Hindu College in Dhab Khatikan. Hans Raj, an aide to Dr Kitchlew, announced that a public protest meeting would be held at 4.30 p.m. the following day in Jallianwala Bagh. A series of resolutions protesting the Rowlatt Act, the actions of the British authorities, and the detention of Dr Satya Pal and Dr Kitchlew were drawn up and approved, after which the meeting was adjourned.

The date had been chosen because it was Baisakhi the next day, the Punjabi New Year.

THE JALLIANWALA MASSACRE

Martial law was imposed on Amritsar and its suburbs from 9 a.m. onwards on Baisakhi, even though it wasn't sanctioned by the Viceroy. Dyer marched through the streets with a notice: 'It is hereby proclaimed to all persons it may concern that no person residing in the city is permitted or allowed to leave the city in his own private or hired conveyance or on foot, without a pass...No person residing in Amritsar City is permitted to leave his house after 8 p.m. Any person found in the streets after 8 p.m. is liable to be shot. No procession of any kind is permitted to parade the streets in the city or any part of the city or outside of it at any time. Any such procession or any gathering of four men will be looked upon and treated as an unlawful assembly and dispersed by force of arms if necessary.'[1]

On that fateful day, Dyer had at his disposal 407 British and 739 Indian soldiers, as well as two armoured cars and several machine guns. During the proclamation, he was accompanied by a detachment of British troops, a contingent of police officials including the deputy commissioner, the superintendent and the deputy superintendent, and the

---

1 Colvin, Ian, *The Life of General Dyer*, London: William Blackwood & Sons Ltd., 1929, p 168.

tehsildar of Amritsar. A man beating a drum drew the attention of the people to the announcement.

The proclamation was read out in English, Urdu, Hindi and Punjabi. Although it was read at 19 different points in the city, both the Hunter Commissions findings and the Congress report mention that it was not read at Jallianwala Bagh or the Golden Temple. The reasons are unclear; after all, the crowds were the largest in these two areas. By not doing so, Dyer failed to inform more than half of the populace and those residing in the most crowded parts of the city about the curfew and the ban on public gatherings. At the same time, a boy was running through the streets of Amritsar beating a tin can shouting that a meeting will be held at Jallianwala Bagh and that local leaders and lawyer Lala Kanhya Lal would preside.

Jallianwala Bagh, close to the Golden Temple, is a large, irregular quadrangle six to seven acres large, approximately 200 x 200 yards in size, and surrounded by walls roughly 10 feet tall. Homes three to four storeys high overlook the Bagh. The main entrance was a narrow passage but not wide enough for a vehicle to pass through. There were no other regular entrances but it was possible to get in through narrow openings at four points. During the monsoons, crops were planted in the Bagh. The rest of the year, it was a local meeting point and playground.

The Bagh began to fill up by early afternoon on 13 April 1919. The local criminal investigation department (CID) had received word of the meeting through word of mouth and plainclothes detectives wandering in the crowds. At 12.45 p.m., Dyer was informed of the meeting.

He returned to his base around 1.30 p.m. to decide how to handle it. 'I had to think the matter out. I had to organise my forces and make up my mind as to where I would put my pickers. I thought I had done enough to make the crowd not meet. If they were going to meet, I had to consider it a military situation and make up my mind what to do, which took me a certain amount of time.'[2]

It must be noted that he did not prevent the meeting from happening. Though both Dyer and Deputy Commissioner Irving, the senior civil authority in Amritsar, were aware of the meeting, they did not inform the people gathered in the Bagh about the curfew and the ban on public gatherings. They did not send the police to disband the crowd. Dyer later said he did not take any action to disperse the crowd as 'I did not think they would meet after all I had done in the morning. I did not think of sending another force to warn them not to go'.[3]

By mid-afternoon, thousands of Sikhs, Muslims and Hindus had gathered. Many had earlier visited the Golden Temple and were passing through the Bagh on their way home. Apart from pilgrims, Amritsar had filled up over the preceding days with farmers, traders and merchants who had come to attend the annual Baisakhi horse and cattle fair. After the city police closed the fair at 2 p.m., farmers drifted into the Bagh and the Golden Temple complex in large numbers. By early afternoon, estimates suggest there were 20,000–25,000 people gathered at the

---

[2] EIllahi, Shereen Fatima, *Empire of Violence - Strategies of British Rule in India and Ireland in the Aftermath of the Great War, Austin*, USA: University of Texas at Austin, 2008, p 61, *Hunter Report: Dyer's Oral Evidence*, Volume 3.

[3] *Congress Report on the Punjab Disorders*, p 59.

Bagh. This included many young boys and infants. No one carried sticks or any form of weaponry. Most of the participants were not there to agitate or cause any chaos or trouble. They were there to celebrate the new year, to wish each other and to meet friends. Shortly after 2 p.m., Dyer sent an aircraft to fly over the Bagh and estimate the size of the crowd.

At around 4 p.m., the meeting protesting the arrests of Dr Kitchlew and Dr Pal began. Speakers suggested a petition be presented to the Lieutenant Governor or the Viceroy for their release. Those gathered nearby drifted towards the speakers to listen.

After J.F. Rehill, Superintendent of Police, confirmed to Dyer that the meeting was indeed taking place, Dyer arrived at the Bagh at about 4.30 p.m. in a convoy of open cars carrying Captain Morgan, Captain Briggs, Rehill and DSP Plomer, preceded by two policemen on horseback. Ninety armed soldiers – carrying 25 rifles from the 9th Gurkhas Regiment and 25 rifles from detachments of 54th Sikhs FF and 59th Sikhs FF – accompanied them.[4] The riflemen were armed with .303 Lee–Enfield bolt-action rifles. It is not clear whether Dyer had specifically chosen troops from the Gurkha Regiment due to their proven loyalty to the British or because they were simply the units readily available. Dyer had also brought two armoured cars armed with machine guns. The vehicles were left outside, unable to enter the Bagh. The ground by the entrance stood at a slightly higher level than the rest. It was from

---

4   Colvin, Ian, *The Life of General Dyer*, London: William Blackwood & Sons Ltd., 1929, p 174; *Congress Report on the Punjab Disorders*, p 59.

this elevated platform that Dyer surveyed the crowd. The soldiers marched in a double file and were positioned at the elevated platform at the entrances – 25 to the right and 25 to the left on the north side of the rectangular space. Stationing his troops thus, he effectively foreclosed any possibility of a quick escape. As the main entrance was relatively wider, it was heavily guarded by troops with machine guns backed by armoured vehicles. Dyer admitted that if he could have taken the armoured vehicles inside, he would have, and the number of casualties would have been higher.

The people inside the Bagh did not know they had been boxed in like caged animals. When the soldiers first arrived, the crowd turned to look at them. Those with children on their shoulders lowered them. Hans Raj, who had arranged for the meeting, entreated the men to stay calm as the soldiers would not fire at innocent people. He ran to the soldiers waving a white flag to indicate the meeting was peaceful.

But Dyer had already made up his mind. Without any warning to disperse, Dyer gave the order to fire. When the firing commenced, Hans Raj shouted to the crowd that the soldiers were shooting blanks; he could not believe they would shoot at unarmed innocents.[5] It was only after he saw people drop to the ground bleeding that he, along with Soham Lal, a baker, made a dash towards a tiny passage between the walls of two homes. They jumped over the wall and escaped.

The troops continued to fire, ordered to shoot directly into the gathering. They kept firing for about 10 minutes, until their supply of 1,650 rounds of ammunition was

---

5   Furneax, Rupert, *Massacre at Amritsar*, London: George Allen Unwin Ltd., 1963, p 13

exhausted. Dyer's justification was stated in his report: 'I realised that my force was small and to hesitate might induce attack. I immediately opened fire and dispersed the mob. I estimate that between 200 and 300 of the crowd were killed.'[6]

Dyer's intentions were made clear subsequently. In 1920, he stated to Major General Sir William Beynon, General Officer Commanding the 16th Division, Lahore, that he had gone to the Bagh with the intention of firing upon the crowd. When Dyer was asked when he gave the orders to fire, he said, 'At once.'[7] He decided to order his troops to fire within 30 seconds of his arrival at the Bagh as his orders had been disobeyed and he wanted to teach the 'rebels' a lesson. He agreed the possibility that some were not aware of the ban on public gatherings existed. '[But] I thought it was my duty to go on until they had dispersed. If I fired a little I should be wrong in firing at all.'[8]

There were also reports that Dyer, from time to time, 'checked his fire and directed it upon places where the crowd was thickest'.[9] He admitted later that he 'had made up his mind to punish them for disobedience for having assembled there'.[10] When a few soldiers initially shot in the air, an annoyed Dyer yelled at them to fire low to ensure maximum casualties. They began to shoot low in the next volley, killing and wounding hundreds. Many in the crowd were trampled in the rush to escape. Witness accounts

---

6   Lloyd, Nick, *The Amritsar Massacre: The Untold Story of One Fateful Day*, I.B. Tauris, 2011, p 176.

7   *Congress Report on the Punjab Disorders*, p 60.

8   *Hunter Report: Dyer's Oral Evidence.*

9   *Hunter Report: Dyer's Written Evidence*, Volume 3, p 61.

10   *Report of Commissions*, Volume 1, II, Mumbai: 1920.

recounted a scene of indescribable horror. Ram Saran Singh, a witness to the Congress fact-finding committee, said he was going to run when an old Sikh told him to lie flat on the ground. Another participant, Pratap Singh, pulled his son down and lay over him while bullets whizzed above him. Those who tried to climb the walls were methodically shot down. Lala Ramgopal was fortunate to scramble over a pile of dead bodies and climb over a wall to safety, but in the process he lost his dhoti and ran down a side street naked. A street trader called Mian Mohammed Sharif was hit on the thigh by a bullet. On seeing another person trying to climb the wall ahead of him, Sharif jumped on top of him, scampered over and escaped. When he reached a passage in the wall, Seth Lakm Chand, another participant, found it blocked by corpses. When he tried to climb over them, he was shot in the leg and lost consciousness. His leg had to be amputated. Moulvi Gholam Jilani said, 'I ran towards a wall and fell on a mass of dead and wounded persons. Many others fell on me… There was a heap of dead and wounded over me, under and all around me. I thought I was going to die.'[11] Several people threw themselves into a well on the compound to escape the bullets. Unfortunately, those who jumped first drowned under the weight of the people jumping in after them. Three months later, 120 bodies were taken out of the well.

~

---

11   Elllahi, Shereen Fatima, *Empire of Violence - Strategies of British Rule in India and Ireland in the Aftermath of the Great War,* Austin, USA: University of Texas at Austin, 2008, p 59.

Dyer's own testimony revealed he was not remorseful about the massacre. He admitted, 'I think it quite possible that I could have dispersed them perhaps even without firing.' But he didn't do so because 'they would all come back and laugh at me and I considered I would be making myself a fool.'[12] The callousness was made worse when it was found that soldiers had directed their guns towards the exit gates through which the people were escaping. Even those who lay flat on the ground were shot at. Dyer later stated that the purpose of his action was to 'strike terror not only in the city of Amritsar but throughout the Punjab', adding, 'I wanted to reduce their morale – the morale of the rebels.'[13] He believed that by his actions, he had thwarted the possibility of a mutiny similar to that in 1857.

Mohammed Ismail, a butcher who reached the Bagh after the shooting, said, 'Corpses were lying all over. There were some wounded also. My estimate of the persons I saw lying was 1,500... At several places the corpses were 10 or 12 [bodies] thick. I saw some children lying dead... There were in all 16,000 to 20,000 people in the garden including I think about 400–500 children.'[14] Lala Girdhari Lal, an eyewitness who watched the massacre from a house overlooking the Bagh, said, 'I saw hundreds of persons killed on the spot... Even those who lay flat on the ground were shot... No arrangements were made by the authorities

---

12 Elllahi, Shereen Fatima, *Empire of Violence - Strategies of British Rule in India and Ireland in the Aftermath of the Great War, Austin*, USA: University of Texas at Austin, 2008, p 61.
13 Ibid, p 65; *Hunter Report: Dyer's Oral Evidence*.
14 Elllahi, Shereen Fatima, *Empire of Violence - Strategies of British Rule in India and Ireland in the Aftermath of the Great War, Austin*, USA: University of Texas at Austin, 2008, p 60.

to look after the dead or wounded... The dead bodies were of grown-up people and young boys also. Some had their heads cut open, others had eyes shot, and nose, chest, arms, or legs shattered... I think there must have been over 1,000 dead bodies in the garden then... I saw people were hurrying up and many had to leave their dead and wounded [behind], because they were afraid of being fired upon again after 8.00 p.m.'[15]

After the incident, Dyer and his troops marched back, leaving a trail of dead and wounded without any remorse. He was callous enough to state that he had left with no concern for the wounded, who could go to hospitals if they so wished. Taking care of the wounded, he told the Hunter Commission, was not his job.

The wounded could also not be moved as a curfew had been declared, and many more died during the night. Though the official figure given by the British inquiry into the massacre is 379, the number of deaths is disputed to this day. In July 1919, three months after the massacre, officials were tasked with finding the true numbers of lives lost by inviting city residents to volunteer information about the dead. However, many feared that those who volunteered would be identified as having been present at the meeting, and some of the dead may not have had close relations in the area to begin with. When interviewed by the members of the Hunter Committee, a senior civil servant in Punjab admitted that the actual figure could be higher than the official figure. It was later estimated that over 1,000 people

---

15 *Congress Report on the Punjab Disorders*, pp 61-62.

were killed that day, and more than 1,500 had been wounded.

Gerald Wathen, principal of Khalsa College, was in Amritsar that day and was extremely disturbed by what had taken place. The British, fearing retaliation, had begun to take precautions. Around 11.30 p.m., Deputy Commissioner Irving sent a sketchy coded message to Lahore mentioning the day's happenings and stating that about 200 people had been killed. Wathen, however, was upset at the handling of the whole affair and insisted that a more detailed account be sent. Irving obliged; the second note was ready by 1.30 a.m. It stated, 'A meeting had been advertised for 4.30 p.m. that day, and the General had said he would attend it with 100 men. I did not think the meeting would be held, or if held would disperse, so I asked the General to excuse me as I wanted to go to the Fort. I learn that the military found a large meeting of some five thousand men, and opened fire without warning, killing about two hundred. Firing went on for about ten minutes. I went through the city at night with the General, and all was absolutely still. I much regret that I was not present, but when out previously with the military the greatest forbearance had been used in making the people disperse. I had absolutely no idea of the action taken.'[16]

Wathen, along with an Indian Civil Services officer who was visiting Amritsar at the time, drove down to Lahore and woke up a sleeping Sir Michael O'Dwyer at 3 a.m., telling him in an agitated manner that only English soldiers had

---

16 Colvin, Ian, *The Life of General Dyer*, London: William Blackwood & Sons Ltd., 1929, pp 184-185.

fired and that Indians were being shot like rabbits. Wathen demanded the Lieutenant Governor himself go to Amritsar to calm matters, else there could be an uprising. O'Dwyer called in Commissioner Kitchin and Chief Secretary J.P. Thompson, both of whom were still in their pyjamas at that early hour. O'Dwyer resented being told off by a college principal and dismissed his report as alarmist. He then sent a message to Irving complaining of Wathen's disrespect. He also telephoned General Beynon who had heard reports about the shooting at 11.45 p.m. but had not heard from Dyer. Beynon did nothing until the next day when he sent an aircraft to Amritsar to check for further trouble.

The next morning, Beynon received Dyer's report in which it was stated that Dyer was determined he wanted to show Amritsaris that he had sufficient military force to maintain law and order. Beynon in turn told O'Dwyer that Dyer's action had 'crushed the rebellion at its heart – Amritsar.'[17] O'Dwyer concurred with this feeling. Beynon then told O'Dwyer he was conveying his approval of Dyer's actions. O'Dwyer decided to endorse this and Beynon wrote to Dyer: 'Your action correct and Lieutenant Governor approves.'[18]

---

17 O'Dwyer, Michael, *India As I Knew It*, London: Constable & Co Ltd, 1925, p 188.
18 Ibid, p 189.

MARTIAL LAW

On the morning of 20 April 1919, a rumour spread in Gujranwala that a dead calf had been hung from one of the railway bridges near the station, inflaming Hindus. Though it was uncertain who was responsible for this, the general public attributed it to be instigated by British authorities. This belief was further strengthened by the fact that pork had been thrown into a mosque as well.

As a crowd proceeded towards the railway bridge to verify the rumour, a Lahore train to Wazirabad arrived. A *khansama* on the train brought news of what had happened the previous day at Jallianwala Bagh. The train was packed with Baisakhi holiday-makers. On hearing the news, the already angry crowd began to pelt stones at the train to prevent it from leaving. Some attempted to set fire to the bridge just before Gurukul school. Receiving information about the irate crowd and sensing the situation could get serious, the Governor of the Gurukul Lala Rallya Ram, lawyer Labh Singh, pleader Din Muhammad, and a few others rushed to the scene to prevent any further mishap. The Gurukul staff and some others quickly put out the fire on the bridge. A British officer and a few constables there did not help in any way; their indifference was later justified by the Superintendent to the Congress and the

Hunter Commission by saying that it was not the job of the police to put out fires. The crowd then proceeded to Kachi Bridge, which was on the other side of the station. Police Superintendent F.A. Herron tried to disperse the crowds, but instead of using peaceful means, he opened fire, killing several people.

The wounded were taken to a meeting of a few other Indians who were trying to pacify the heightened emotions and keep the people within city limits. Seeing the wounded, however, the meeting broke up and a now furious mob proceeded towards the station, damaging several buildings along the way – the church, the post office, the tehsil office, the court house and the railway station. The police made no attempts to check this incendiarism. The colonel in charge, A.J. O'Brien, asked for assistance. O'Dwyer was told by Beynon that troops could not be sent immediately to Gujranwala and, as a result, he ordered a bombing raid on the city.

Although the crowds had quietened by now, military bombers swooped over the city around 3 p.m. and indiscriminately dropped bombs on random targets such as Khalsa Boarding House, where no meetings had taken place. The boarding house was about half a mile away from the city and more than a mile away from the station where the disturbances had taken place. One of the students at the boarding house heard an aircraft hover over the building at around 3 p.m. for about 10 minutes. The next thing he knew, a bomb tore through the building, instantly killing the confectioner of the hostel. The bomb missed the student, but shrapnel injured his hand. Another young boy fainted due to the shock of the explosion. Following this incident, the superintendent of the boarding house had to reiterate that there had been no political meeting held on their premises, nor were such meetings permitted. He clarified that on 14 April, not one of his boarders had ventured into the city.

A washerboy was killed when a bomb dropped on him near a fountain in the middle of Gujranwala, injuring another 12-year-old child. Schoolchildren were playing in an open field when they saw an aircraft fly so low they could see the men inside drop the bomb a little ahead of them. A farmer was hit by shrapnel while returning after watering his buffaloes. He was treated at a nearby hospital for a month, then arrested for no offence and finally released without trial. People fleeing to villages outside the city were shot at. Bombs were dropped on homes where people had taken refuge – with innocent people inside who had not participated in any mob activity. A total of 12 people were killed and at least 24 were injured in the bombing raid.

The British said the bombing was conducted 'to have a sort of moral effect'. According to British officer Captain Carberry, his orders were 'to disperse crowds going or coming'.[1] That afternoon, Brigadier General NDK MacEwen, Commanding Officer of the Royal Air Force in India, felt he had done a commendable job of quelling the riots in Gujranwala and expertly dispersing the mob by using bombs and Lewis guns.[2] On the other hand, O'Brien

---

1 *Congress Report on Punjab Disorders*, p 121.
2 O'Shea, Joe, *An Account of Murder, Mutiny and Mayhem*, O'Brien Press, 2013.

was of the opinion that more Indians should have been killed.[3]

Meanwhile, O'Dwyer had sent a telegram on 12 April to the Government of India seeking permission to impose martial law. This was sanctioned on 14 April by an ordinance 'whereas the Governor-General is satisfied that a state of open rebellion against the authority of the Government exists in certain parts of the Provinces of the Punjab'[4]. The General Officer Commanding had to act in consultation with O'Dwyer, and he could not disregard any advice given by the latter.[5]

When the imposition of martial law was sought, an article appeared in the *Civil and Military Gazette*, an English-owned and edited paper, a day after the firing, which falsely stated that the order had been given to fire at Jallianwala Bagh because the crowd had refused to disperse. This article was brought to the attention of the Council while they were debating on the imposition of martial law and influenced their decision. On 14 April, the Government also published its Resolution 549, which stated that it would employ its military resources to maintain law and order and that the Governor General would extend his full support to all those responsible for maintaining order. Martial law was proclaimed on 15 April, and it remained in force till 9 June.

In Gujranwala, Colonel O'Brien got the military and the police to indiscriminately arrest barristers, pleaders and

---

3   *Congress Report on Punjab Disorders*, p 123
4   Colvin, Ian, *The Life of General Dyer*, London: William Blackwood & Sons Ltd., 1929, p 188.
5   O'Dwyer, Michael, *India As I Knew It*, London: Constable & Co Ltd, 1925, p 198.

others despite the fact that they had helped control the mobs. To do this, he resorted to the Defence of India Regulation that said, 'In exercise of the powers conferred by Rule 12 A.A. of the Defence of India Consolidation Rules, 1915, the Lieutenant Governor is pleased to authorize all commissioners to arrest without warrant any person against whom reasonable suspicion exists that he is promoting or assisting to promote rebellion against the authority of the Government.'[6] Those arrested included the Governor of the Gurukul, 63-year-old Rallya Ram. They were not even allowed to dress – the reason being that O'Brien was in a hurry to complete the arrests. They were all handcuffed, and each person's handcuff was chained to the next person's handcuff, with one chain passing through all the handcuffs. They were then marched to the railway station, and from there into the city under the hot sun, while an aircraft flew over them and machine guns followed them.

Twenty-two men were arrested during the course of the day. They were made to sit in an open coal truck with 4 policemen and 25 soldiers guarding them. They were refused permission to even answer nature's call, with the soldiers even forcing a man who had urinated in the truck to sit in it. They reached Lahore at 9 p.m. where they were kept in solitary cells. The men were held for 18 days before being taken back to Gujranwala, where they were marched to the railway station once again, this time carrying their mattresses in one hand while the other was cuffed. They were given no food for the whole day. Then, they were

---

6 *Congress Report on Punjab Disorders*, pp 123-124.

detained for another 18 days in Gujranwala, before being brought back to Lahore for their trial by the Martial Law Tribunal. Only five of them were acquitted in the trial.

This was just the beginning of British brutality which was about to get even worse. Perhaps the most humiliating of all the indignities was when Dyer enforced the now-infamous crawling order in Amritsar.

On 19 April, General Dyer met Miss Sherwood, who had earlier been molested in Amritsar. Subsequently, he issued an order that every Indian man using the street on which she had been assaulted must crawl across its length on his hands and knees. This was a verbal order and was withdrawn when the General was told to do so by his superiors. However, the order remained in force for seven days until 25 April.

When questioned by the Hunter Commission as to why he had initiated the crawling order, Dyer dismissively explained that the order only entailed practices that were familiar to the 'natives'. His unbridled contempt for Indians was apparent in his explanation to a British inspector: 'Some Indians crawl face downwards in front of their gods. I wanted them to know that a British woman is as sacred as a Hindu God and therefore they have to crawl in front of her, too… It is a small point, but in fact "crawling order" is a misnomer; the order was to go down on all fours in an attitude well understood by natives of India in relation to holy places.'[7]

---

[7] Talbot, Strobe, *Engaging India: Diplomacy, Democracy and the Bomb,* Washington DC, USA: Brookings Institution, March 2006, p 245; Lal, Vinay, 'The Incident of the "Crawling Lane" – Women in the Punjab Disturbances of 1919', Genders No. 16, Texas: University of Texas Press, 1993

The lane down which Indians were made to crawl was approximately 150 to 200 yards in length, as well as narrow and crowded. There were several two-storeyed houses on either side and many more homes in the alleyways and by-lanes that branched off it. The people living in this locality would necessarily have to use the 'crawling' lane if they stepped out. The crawling order applied to every person who used this lane, despite the fact that most of them had nothing to do with the assault on Miss Sherwood. The blind, the sick and the physically challenged were all required to obey the order. No exceptions were permitted, even if it was for a medical emergency. What Dyer referred to as 'going on all fours' meant that the men had to crawl the length of the lane flat on their bellies. If they lifted their knees or bent their body in any way to relieve the pain, the police would immediately dig their rifle-butts into the backs of the transgressors and force them back into the reptile position.

The order was strictly enforced by the police from 6 a.m. to 8 p.m.; additionally, from 15 April, the hours of the curfew were also extended up to 10 p.m. When asked for a justification for the timings, Dyer dismissively retorted, 'They could leave at all other times.'[8] What he conveniently omitted to mention was that should they do so, they would be breaking the curfew order enforced between 10 p.m. and 6 a.m., for which they could be shot dead.

Witness accounts mentioned in the Congress report and made to the Hunter Commission tell us how the order was enforced and the pains it caused the local populace. Cloth

---

8   *Congress Report on Punjab Disorders*, p 67.

merchant Lala Megha Mal's house was located in Kutcha Kurichan, the 'crawling' lane, and his shop was at Guru Bazaar, a short distance away. The very first day of the order, when Lala Megha Mal was returning home from work at 5 p.m., soldiers stopped him at the entrance to the lane and ordered him to crawl on his belly. Terrified, he managed to run away and escape the soldiers; he then waited till they had left before he stealthily crept back around 9 p.m. When he got home, he discovered that his wife was ill with a fever. There was no water in the house for her to drink, no doctor available and no medicines. He left the house late at night to fetch some water, but for the seven days that the order was in force, he was unable to treat his wife. No doctor would visits patients in the lane they had to crawl through.

Opium contractor Lala Rallya Ram's shop was also located in the lane, and he was compelled to crawl to his shop. Besides the discomfort and distress, he had to bear the indignity of being kicked by soldiers with heavy boots. Not satisfied with just kicks, soldiers would also hit him with their rifle butts. There were days when he did not go back home to eat.

For the full duration of the order, not a single sweeper came to the clear the refuse, nor were the latrines cleaned. The water carriers too stayed away and vegetable vendors also avoided the lane. Lala Rallya Ram's neighbour, Lala Ganpat, suffered the same difficulties. Even those who went to worship at the temple in the lane were required to crawl all the way. Banker Lala Devi Das, on being told to crawl, offered to return home to save himself the indignity. This request was refused and the soldiers threatened him with bayonets to force him to crawl. Kahan Chand, a blind man, was similarly required to crawl and was kicked mercilessly. A teacher, Abdulla, was hit by a rifle butt when he rested midway through the lane. A woman who resided in the lane said that soldiers came into her house when her menfolk were out, beat her servants and then called for her. She practiced purdah and did not appear in public even before servants. But she was made to take off her purdah. Frightened, she complied. She was then asked, under threat, to name who had attacked Miss Sherwood.

Whilst the order was being enforced, sacred pigeons and other birds were shot in the lane. The *pinjarapole* – a sacred house built for the care of animals which was at one end of the lane – was defiled. British soldiers contaminated and polluted the water of several wells in Amritsar, using them as latrines. The soldiers defecated in the only well in the lane.

As though the order was not sufficient, Dyer authorized the indiscriminate public thrashing of Indians who came within a lathi-length of British policemen. To facilitate flogging, a flogging-booth ('*tiktiki*') was built and prominently positioned in the middle of the lane. Dyer wanted to ensure that those who were suspected of assaulting Miss Sherwood were properly punished and, therefore, had them lashed in public. Six boys were flogged at this specially constructed flogging booth. They were tied to the post and given 30 lashes. One of the boys, Sundar Singh, lost consciousness after the fourth lash, but as he had not completed his punishment, he was doused with water and allowed a few sips to revive himself, and the remaining lashes were administered once he had regained consciousness. Unable to bear the pain, Sundar Singh once again lost consciousness. The soldiers continued to flog him till he had been lashed 30 times. The other boys were similarly treated. After the flogging, they were then handcuffed and, as they could not walk, were dragged by the police to the fort.

Under martial law, Indians were ordered to salute all British officers. The *'salaam* order' was imposed almost universally in Punjab, and refusal was met with punishment. On 18 April, Lala Har Gopal Khanna saluted Dyer and some policemen on horseback in the military manner with the wrong hand. Dyer told him to report the next day. When Khanna asked the Deputy Superintendent of Police Plomer where he should report, Plomer told a policeman to take Khanna to the police station, where he was made to squat on a damp floor with a few others. At dusk several others joined them and they were made to squat the whole night in the open with a Gurkha soldier watching over them. At 8.30 a.m. the next day, they were taken to a ground and made to stand in the hot sun until a military sergeant came and taught them how they were expected to *salaam*. Only then were they allowed to leave.

The following Martial Law notice that was issued in Gujranwala shows the extent of the *salaam* order[9]:

---

9   *Congress Report on Punjab Disorders*, p 125.

MARTIAL LAW NOTICE NO. 7

We have come to know that Gujranwala district inhabitants do not usually show respect to the gazetted commissioners, European civil and military officers of His Imperial Majesty, by which the prestige and honour of the Government is not maintained. Therefore we order that the inhabitants of Gujranwala district should show proper respect to these respectable officers, whenever they have occasion to meet them, in the same way as big and rich people of India are respected.

Whenever anyone is on horseback or is driving any kind of wheeled conveyance, he must get down. One who has opened or got an umbrella in his hand, should close or lower it down, and all these persons should salute with their right hand respectfully.

(Sd.) L.W.Y. CAMPBELL,
BRIG.–GENERAL,
OFFICER COMMANDING, DISTRICT
GUJRANWALA

Campbell zealously took the order a step further and outlined the exact manner in which 'respect to the gazetted commissioners, European civil and military officers of His Imperial Majesty' should be shown so that 'the prestige and honour of the Government' could be maintained. All 160,000 inhabitants of Gujranwala were required to obey the order precisely and if the salute did not meet the standards of the British officer, the punishment was severe. If a person did not *salaam* an Englishman by mistake or oversight, he had his turban taken off his head and tied around his neck. He was then dragged to the military camp where he was either fined or flogged. One person was even made to kiss the boots of an officer because his *salaam* had not been noticed.

As though the torture was not sufficient, the British took to humiliating respected persons of the town. Men of status were made to clean the drains. Lawyers were made to act as coolies and to patrol the street in the hot sun as punishment for taking part in public affairs and agitating against the Rowlatt Act. Lawyer Balmokand Bhatia said he was made to patrol the city and gardens the whole day while soldiers contemptuously referred to him as a mere constable. There were times he was made to work as a coolie carrying furniture while the orderlies and other staff, who normally did this work, were made to watch. The punishment for not fulfilling these duties diligently was flogging, but could also be imprisonment or even death. At least 93 lawyers were humiliated in a similar manner, often in the presence of people who held them in high regard and respect. A 75-year-old lawyer named Lala Kanhya Lal was forced to act as a special constable and, despite his advanced age, was made to carry furniture from one place to another and to patrol the city under the hot sun.

Another form of torture was to paste notices on the houses of those considered to be 'evilly disposed persons'.[10] The residents of the building were made responsible for any damage done to the notices. This devilish scheme was administered by Colonel Johnson, Martial Law Administrator in Lahore, who felt this was apt punishment for those the C.I.D. considered disloyal to the Empire.

---

10 *Congress Report on Punjab Disorders*, p 95.

Safeguarding these notices under a 24-hour watch was, he felt, a most appropriate and justifiable punishment for the offenders.

The Sanatan Dharma College in Lahore was selected as one of the buildings to put up such a notice. When the notice was torn down by unknown persons, the British officer in charge ordered the arrest of every male on the premises. Five hundred students and professors were arrested and marched to the fort three miles away, while carrying their bedding on their shoulders in the hot sun. They were released within two days after the principal undertook an assurance that the notices would be preserved. Other students were hounded as well. Students of DAV College, Dyal Singh College and Medical College were, to 'keep them out of mischief', made to appear for roll call four times a day – at 7 a.m. and 11 a.m., and at 3 p.m. and 7 p.m. The Medical College students had to walk 17 miles every day in the scorching sun of Lahore to do this. All students were required to salute the Union Jack.

Colonel Johnson tried to make it appear as if a state of war existed in the Punjab. Those who broke the curfew order knowingly or unknowingly were publicly whipped. He also said that if any bomb was thrown on his soldiers, he would take it to assume it was done by all persons standing within a 100-yard radius; consequently, he would have all those living in that area vacate their homes and shops in an hour. He would then annihilate every building there except the mosques and temples. He commandeered 200 *tongas* and all motor cars belonging to Indians until the martial law was revoked in July 1919. All free restaurants were closed down and the prices of food items were regulated. Johnson himself tried cases in summary courts he constituted and convicted 201 persons out of the 207 he tried, with sentences ranging from fines and flogging to two-year imprisonments.

Johnson's Notice was directed at munshis, agents and *chaprasi*s (peons) of pleaders who were accused of being involved in disseminating seditious propaganda. None of them could leave Lahore without a permit, while their employers had to submit a list of their employees every month. He also issued an order making it a crime for more than two Indians to walk abreast. Indians were also always made to give way to a European. On one occasion, a marriage party was arrested because there were more than 10 persons accompanying the groom. The bridegroom, priest and some others of the party were flogged.

People were forbidden to carry sticks. Railway travel was stopped and the people were reduced to a state of helplessness. In Gujranwala, martial order rule 2 stated that if shopkeepers refused to sell articles to the army or police or if they kept their shops shut, they'd be arrested and liable to be flogged. Soldiers were reported to take butter from houses without making any payment. When this was stopped, every house (other than those of widows) was required to pay one rupee towards the expenses of the military. Beds were taken from houses without any payment. To avoid harassment, bribes were given to policemen who happily accepted them. On 18 April, a train arrived at Nizamabad, a small village near Wazirbad, bearing a troop of soldiers who surrounded the village and ransacked the shops.

When telegraph wires were cut, mobile units were sent under Major Braid to investigate and punish those responsible. A large number of persons were taken hostage to put pressure on others to provide information. S.M. Jacob, Director of Agriculture, took six hostages from one village, but the *lambardar* did not show any inclination to help nor did he give any information. Although he had no authority to conduct a summary court trial, Jacob had the *lambardar* stripped to his loincloth, tied to a tree and given 15 stripes with a cane. He was also fined Rs 200. In Kasur, orders were given by Colonel Doveton that those who had left their homes on or after 10 April should return or else their properties would be confiscated. Six homes were thus visited and the clothes and vessels therein were burnt and destroyed. On 1 May, the whole town excluding women and children was ordered to report to the railway station to be identified. Kasur residents had to sit bareheaded in the sun till 2 p.m. without food or water. Search parties were sent to ensure that there were no absentees. Additionally, trials were held for those suspected to be involved in subversive activities. Forty men were sentenced to be whipped. The total number of stripes to be given was 710. The flogging post was erected on the station platform. During this time, a headmaster reported that his boys were getting insubordinate and asked for military help. The Commanding Officer decided that they, too, should be whipped. The boys were collected and the headmaster was asked to choose six boys. Three boys from the complaining school and three boys from another school were selected for no other reason than the fact that they were bodily fit to receive the punishment. They were whipped outside the station entrance in front of the other boys.

Meanwhile, none of this information had been transmitted to the rest of the country. Punjab had been completely disconnected after press censorship was introduced on 11 April 1919 and Indian papers had to stop publication. Only the *Civil and Military Gazette* was permitted to publish news, all of which was fabricated. Another English-owned paper, *The Pioneer*, published the lie that the Amritsar crowd had attacked the British at Jallianwala Bagh and was repulsed. The false article in the *Civil and Military Gazette* was published while discussions were ongoing in Delhi as to whether martial law should be imposed and was, in part, responsible for the law being enforced.

The Hindu, the leading newspaper in Madras, was served with a notice to show cause as its editor had presided over a meeting at which Govardhan Das, a resident of Lahore, gave a first-hand account of martial law in the Punjab. The notice asked why the newspaper should not be called upon to furnish a security of Rs 2,000. Das was arrested on a warrant issued by the Punjab Government and sentenced to three years' rigorous imprisonment. Apart from news, even outside counsel such as Motilal Nehru were not permitted into the Punjab to defend those accused because authorities in Punjab felt confident about being able to control local lawyers, while those from outside could not be relied upon.

Nair, who was member of the Viceroy's Council then, had agreed to the imposition of martial law. He, too, had been misled by the false report that had appeared in the *Civil and Military Gazette*. He had hoped that martial law would bring an end to the bloodshed and violence. He had not contemplated the excesses of the British.

However, he gradually started receiving reports from Amritsar, Lahore and other places of the brutality and killings by the British. Additionally, in his capacity as an Indian on the Viceroy's Council, Nair began receiving eyewitness reports of the massacre at Jallianwala Bagh and of the horrors perpetrated by the British under the guise of martial law. The disproportionate severity of the punishments, the callous and unmindful destruction of human life, and the humiliation and agony of a people rendered completely helpless were unimaginable for him. In his autobiography, he writes, 'If to govern the country, it is necessary that innocent persons should be slaughtered at Jallianwala Bagh, and that any civilian officer may, at any time, call in the military, and the two together may butcher the people of Jallianwala Bagh, the country is not worth living in.'[11]

---

11 Nair, C. Sankaran, *Autobiography of C. Sankaran Nair*, Chennai: Lady Madhavan Nair, 1966, p 386.

BACKLASH

Those in power in the Punjab had attempted to portray their orders as imperatives to ensure that there would not be a repeat of the 1857 uprising. Lord Chelmsford recommended to O'Dwyer that press messages should be edited and no mentions should appear about atrocities such as flogging as far as possible[1]. O'Dwyer was also told that reports of people being suppressed would be harmful to the image of English rule in India. After ensuring that Indian papers could not be printed, English editors such as Benjamin Horniman of the *Bombay Chronicle*, who had written against the Government, were deported. The Government regularly sent a communication titled 'Report on the Native Papers' to the Secretary of State in London. This, too, did not make any mention of the Jallianwala Bagh massacre.[2] As a consequence, O'Dwyer and Dyer were lauded as heroes in England for their timely and courageous actions to save the Empire.

But the truth finally did trickle through, and Indians were appalled at the callous manner in which innocents had been massacred in Jallianwala Bagh and the horrors

---

1 Kaul, Chandrika, *Reporting the Raj: The British Press and India*, Manchester: University Press, 2003, p 207.
2 Ibid.

of martial law. These were viewed as yet another clear indication of British racialism. Political intelligentsia now lost faith in British justice and rule, as did the rest of the populace. There was a sense of intense outrage across India.

Secretary of State for India Edwin Montagu was, at this time, in London and had not really appreciated the enormity of the horrors of Jallianwala Bagh and the Punjab because he had not been given the entire story. The Government in India had only forwarded Deputy Commissioner Irving's initial report that there had been 200 casualties. Lord Chelmsford even stated that the 'effect was salutary'.[3] However, Montagu received disturbing reports from newspapers published outside the Punjab such as the *Bombay Chronicle* and he asked the Viceroy for more information on the shooting in Amritsar, the imposition of martial law and the manner in which it was imposed. Chelmsford sent a telegram to Montagu on 21 May 1919 with the estimates of casualties at Delhi, Amritsar, Lahore, Ahmedabad and Calcutta, mentioning that about six or nine Europeans and about 400 Indians were dead. He was also told about the imposition of martial law and the crawling order.

Chelmsford's detailed report dated 7 May, which Montagu received on 8 June 1919, upset him. The crawling order was particularly obnoxious. He immediately telegraphed the Viceroy: 'Dyer's judgement and temper have in my opinion proved so unreliable that I am of the opinion that he cannot be fit to retain command. I consider

---

3 Collett, Nigel, *The Butcher of Amritsar: Brigader General Reginald Dyer,* London: Hambledon Continuum, 2006, p 323.

it very undesirable that he should continue in the army of India…I think you should relieve him of his command and send him to England.'[4]

Lord Chelmsford, aware of how popular Dyer was with the army and Britishers in India, said Dyer's prompt action had saved the Empire. 'I was extremely sorry to get your telegram with regard to Dyer, not that I think it was unnatural in the circumstances… I have heard that Dyer administered Martial Law in Amritsar very reasonably and in no sense tyrannously. In these circumstances you will understand why it is that both the Commander-in-Chief and I feel very strongly that an error of judgement, transitory in nature, should not bring down upon him a penalty which would be out of proportion to the offence which must be balanced against very notable services which he rendered at an extremely critical time.'[5]

Montagu's reaction to this telegram shows his concern. 'I have again deferred on this matter to your opinion. I should not have complained if Dyer had lynched those who attacked the lady missionary. It was the savage and inappropriate folly of the order which roused my anger… I cannot admit that any service Dyer has rendered anywhere can atone for action of this kind, and I am very much worried that he should escape punishment for an order, the results of which are likely to be permanent.'[6]

---

[4] Kaul, Chandrika, *Reporting the Raj: The British Press and India*, Manchester: University Press, 2003, p 207

[5] Collett, Nigel, *The Butcher of Amritsar: Brigader General Reginald Dyer,* London: Hambledon Continuum, 2006, p 323.

[6] Ibid, p 324.

Meanwhile, the All India Congress Committee passed a resolution in Allahabad on 8 June demanding an enquiry into the actions of the British and requested Sankaran Nair to go to London to lobby for one. Nair was increasingly uncomfortable and disillusioned by the events in the Punjab, especially when he discovered that Lord Chelmsford had, in fact, approved of the actions of the British Government. 'That to me was shocking.'[7] Sir Nair wanted to resign from the Viceroy's Council, but was dissuaded by Charles Freer Andrews, an influential priest and friend of Mahatma Gandhi, Annie Besant, Motilal Nehru and others. They wanted him to advance India's cause from within the Council in which he was the only Indian member.

Andrews had been a priest of the Church of England who had come to India as a missionary. He had instead fallen in love with the country. After meeting Indian leaders and seeing the plight of Indians, he became an active supporter of the Indian nationalist movement. Nair asked Andrews to meet Lord Chelmsford and seek his permission to visit Lahore, then capital of the Punjab. But when Andrews met with Lord Chelmsford and broached the matter of martial law excesses, the Viceroy flew into an apoplectic rage and asked him whether Indians had now realized what it meant to goad an Englishman. On hearing this, Sir Nair became even more determined to resign but Andrews requested him to continue until he returned from Lahore. Unfortunately,

---

7   Menon, K.P.S., *C. Sankaran Nair: Builders of Modern India*, New Delhi: Publication Division, Ministry of Information and Broadcasting, 1974, pp 136-137.

Andrews was arrested on his way to Lahore and sent back ignominiously.

Nair thus resigned from the Viceroy's Executive Council on 23 July. Soon after, he was called in by Lord Chelmsford for a final interview to the Viceregal Lodge. As soon as he entered the mock-Tudor palace designed by Henry Irwin, he was escorted to the Viceroy's study. A giant portrait of the monarch was placed above the impressive, perfectly polished mahogany table and dominated the room. The Viceroy rose from a straight-backed but ornate maroon velvet-upholstered chair embossed with the imposing crest of the British Empire, and gestured for him to sit on another equally ornate chair in front of him. This was not an occasion that involved the exchange of pleasantries.

Once they had both settled into their chairs, Lord Chelmsford politely expressed his regret on receiving Nair's resignation. Then, with no real interest in Sir Nair's opinion but with typical British courtesy, the Viceroy enquired whether Sir Nair could suggest someone as a successor. Sir Nair, sensing the Viceroy's disinterest and unconcern for anything an Indian had to suggest, found it hard to resist one last dig. Looking directly at the Viceroy and speaking in a solemn tone, as though he had given this matter very serious thought, he said, 'Yes' and pointed to the turbaned, red- and gold-liveried peon standing ramrod straight by the giant doorway. Sir Nair, still perfectly straight-faced, continued, 'That man there, Ram Parshad.'

Lord Chelmsford almost shot out of his chair. Nair replied, 'Why not? He is tall. He is handsome. He wears his livery well and he will say yes to whatever you say. Altogether he will make an ideal Member of Council.'[8] Leaving the Viceroy speechless, Sir Nair warmly shook his hand and quietly exited the chambers.

Nair's resignation stunned the nation, the immediate outcome of which was press censorship in Punjab getting lifted in three days. O'Dwyer announced four days after Sir Nair's resignation that martial law would be terminated, and it was so done within a fortnight. Shocked after Nair's resignation, Montagu now asked Chelmsford to hold an inquiry on the Punjab disturbances. The Viceroy reluctantly agreed and the Hunter Committee was set up in October 1919, to be chaired by Lord William Hunter, a Senator of the College of Justice of Scotland. Its purpose was to determine what exactly had transpired in Amritsar and in other parts that year. Four of its members were British and three were Indians, namely:

1. Lord William Hunter: Chairman of the Committee, ex-Solicitor-General and Senator of the College of Justice in Scotland;
2. W.F. Rice: Additional Secretary to the Government of India (Home Department);
3. Justice G.C. Rankin: Judge of the High Court, Calcutta;
4. Major General Sir George Barrow: Commandant of the Peshawar Division, a non-official Englishman;
5. Thomas Smith: Member of the Legislative Council of the Deputy Governor of the United Provinces;

---

8   Menon, K.P.S., *C. Sankaran Nair: Builders of Modern India*, New Delhi: Publication Division, Ministry of Information and Broadcasting, 1974, pp 136-137

6. Sir Chimanlal Setalvad: Vice-Chancellor of Bombay University and Advocate of the Bombay High Court;
7. Pandit Jagat Narayan: Member of the Legislative Council of the Deputy Governor of the United Provinces;
8. Sardar Sahibzada Sultan Ahmed Khan, Muntazim–ud-doula: Member for Appeals, Gwalior State.

While giving him the brief on the commission, Montagu told Hunter, 'You might find men and newspapers anxious to lead you past alleys which you should explore in order that you may be prevailed upon to "whitewash".'[9] Hunter was told that the Government had nothing to fear from a searching inquiry and that its purpose was to restore public confidence and to present the truth to the world.

After convening in Delhi on 29 October, the committee met and interviewed witnesses in Delhi for eight days, in Ahmedabad for six days, in Bombay for three days and in Lahore for 29 days. With the exception of O'Dwyer and three others who gave their evidence *in camera*, all others gave their evidence in public. Even though the committee was not a court of law and witnesses were not questioned under oath, the members were successful, by rigorous cross-examination, to get detailed accounts. As these meetings were held in public, they were reported extensively in papers both in India and in England.

Montagu, on reading these reports, was concerned and wanted a parliamentary committee constituted. He invited Nair to London to give evidence before the parliamentary

---

9   Kaul, Chandrika, *Reporting the Raj: The British Press and India*, Manchester: University Press, 2003, p 208.

committee. Delighted to have the opportunity to present the facts, Nair readily agreed as he was determined to ensure that an incident as horrific as the Jallianwala Bagh massacre never occurred again.

Prior to his departure, Nair had a conversation with Lord Chelmsford. When he mentioned that he was visiting London on Montagu's request, Chelmsford promptly informed the latter that there really was no need to invite Nair who was in any case planning on visiting London at his own expense, ensuring that Nair would not be accorded any of the benefits of being a guest of the Government. He would also have to pay his own passage money.

But expense was certainly not going to stop Sir Nair. He arrived in London a few days after the evidence of Dyer was reported in the *Pioneer*, where Dyer had testified to the commission that he had planned the shooting at Jallianwala Bagh in advance and that it was intended not just to disband and scatter the crowd but to produce a 'moral impact' across the country. More damning was his admission that he would have used machine guns and armoured cars if it had been possible. He finally admitted to the commission that he had made the decision to abandon the wounded, leaving them there to die.

Sir Nair brought Dyer's admissions to the attention of John Robertson, editor of the *Westminster Gazette*, whose article the next day 'created a sensation all over England'.[10] Another *Times* article asked, 'How comes it that a British general can inflict nearly 2000 casualties on an unarmed

---

10 Nair, C. Sankaran, *Autobiography of C. Sankaran Nair*, Chennai: Lady Madhavan Nair, 1966, p 388.

mob in the Punjab, without the full facts being forwarded within a reasonable time by the Viceroy to the Secretary of State? We have examined the whole of the Viceroy's reports as transmitted to the Press in this country for publication, and they contain very little indication of what happened at Amritsar on the day in question.'[11] The *Morning Post,* which had been a staunch supporter of Dyer, regretted that the British public had been kept in the dark on what had actually transpired.

When Nair forwarded his critical views on Dyer to Montagu, the latter wondered whether he would enter Parliament. Nair mentioned that he was not interested. A few days later, Montagu offered Nair a seat on the Council of the Secretary of State for India. Knowing that he could work for the benefit of India, Nair accepted and became a member on 2 January 1920.

The Government of India's dispatch on the Punjab disturbances, which came a few days after Nair's appointment, was referred to the Secretary of State's council for its opinion. All the members other than Nair accepted the government's view. Sir Nair submitted a separate report asking for the events in the Punjab to be condemned. This report was submitted to the cabinet which discussed it at length but no action was taken as the British were doing exactly the same in Ireland whose people were also putting up a fight for independence from Great Britain.

In the meantime, the Congress had brought out its own report prior to the release of the Hunter Commission's

---

11 Kaul, Chandrika, *Reporting the Raj: The British Press and India*, Manchester: University Press, 2003, p 211.

findings, which was yet to be published. Chelmsford was worried about the effect the Congress's report would have in Britain and he hoped Montagu could persuade the press to hold its publication in England for a while or at least try to influence the press to not comment on the report. Chelmsford had also received an advance copy of the Hunter report, in which the Indian members of the committee expressed disagreement with their English counterparts over the findings.

Chelmsford now conceded that Dyer had acted inhumanely and discussed the Hunter report with Commander-in-Chief Sir Munro, who was already upset with Dyer for the crawling order and for lying to him by not admitting it had been his idea. Because Dyer was being seen as the person who had averted another mutiny, it was decided he could not be court martialled or dismissed. However, he was to be removed from India. He was relieved of his command while recuperating in Jalandhar during his sick leave.

In early March, Dyer received a telegram asking him to meet Munro in Delhi on 9 March. As doctors would not permit him to travel, the date was changed to 23 March. On that day, Munro told Dyer that it would not be possible for him to command troops in India any longer and that he would not be reinstated or taken back in any capacity into service in India. Dyer was told to return to England on sick leave. He had no choice but to accept this. Dyer finally left India on 10 April 1920. His recommendation for a Commander of the British Empire (CBE) title for his services in the Third Afghan War was also withdrawn.

The Hunter Committee report was finally issued on 8 March, and a summary of the report was published by Reuters in the beginning of April. The India Office received a copy on 7 April along with despatches of the Government of India. The report was unusual in that members disagreed in several instances, possibly because of racial differences. Indian members stood their ground and did not permit their English counterparts to stifle their views. As a result, when the six volumes of evidence was finally released in March 1920, there were two reports, a Majority Report signed by the chairman and the four English members, and a Minority Report signed by the three Indian Members.

With regard to the events before 13 April, the committee was in agreement with the action taken to suppress the disorder. The English members regarded the firing on 10 April in Amritsar after the arrest of Satya Pal and Kitchlew as justified on account of the excesses that followed such as the killing of English bank managers and the assault on Miss Sherwood. However, the Indians disagreed and held that the excesses occurred due to the firing on a crowd that had no intention of being violent.

Both the reports condemned the massacre at Jallianwala Bagh. They condemned Dyer's decision to not give notice to disperse, opening fire without warning, and continuing to fire after the crowd had begun to disperse. The report said, 'In continuing to fire as long as he did it appears to us that General Dyer committed a grave error.'[12] The committee found General Dyer exceeded the reasonable

---

12 *The Hunter Committee Report.*

requirements of the case and showed a misconception of duty which resulted in a lamentable and unnecessary loss of life. It regretted that no action was taken by civil or military authorities to remove the dead and their failure to give aid to the wounded. The report also stated that the Government of India agreed with the committee that General Dyer should have given adequate warning before opening fire.

While the Majority Report felt a state of rebellion had existed and consequently the imposition of martial law was correct, the Minority Report disagreed. According to them, the disturbances had not amounted to a rebellion and these could have been controlled and order restored without bringing in the military. The Minority Report also stated that there was no conspiracy to overthrow British rule. Both reports condemned the *salaam* order, the crawling order, the public floggings and the excesses during the martial order. O'Dwyer was criticized by stating that 'he would have acted more wisely if before expressing any approval of General Dyer's action, on this occasion, he had taken steps to ascertain the facts and circumstances of the firing more fully'.[13]

The Minority Report further added:
1. The proclamations in Amritsar prohibiting public meetings were not adequately distributed.
2. There was no violence in Jallianwala Bagh and that there were innocent people in the crowd.
3. General Dyer should have ensured that the wounded were cared for.

---

13 *The Hunter Committee Report.*

4. Dyer's actions had 'by adopting an inhuman and un-British method of dealing with subjects of his Majesty the King Emperor done great disservice to the interest of British Rule in India'.[14]

Even though the committee's findings had been damning, the Hunter Committee did not impose any penal or disciplinary action because Dyer's actions were condoned by his immediate superiors. In fact, General William Beynon was a staunch supporter of Dyer. The Legal and Home Members on the Viceroy's Council finally decided that despite Dyer acting in a heartless and cruel manner, no action should be taken against him for political reasons. In any case, Chelmsford's report to the India office had advised that Dyer had been removed from Indian service and that he was returning to England on sick leave.

On reading the commission report, Montagu was concerned. He persuaded the cabinet to appoint a committee to consider and advise on the Hunter Commission's findings. This committee included Lord Birkenhead, the Lord Chancellor; Ian MacPherson, the Chief Secretary for Ireland; and Winston Churchill, the Secretary of State for War.

Contrary to Dyer's statements to the committee, when he arrived in England on 2 May, he told a *Daily Mail* reporter, 'I shot to save the British Raj – to preserve India for the Empire and protect English men and English women who looked to me for protection. And now I am told to go for doing my duty – my horrible dirty duty… I had to shoot. I had thirty

---

14 *The Hunter Committee Report.*

seconds to make up my mind what action to take and I did it. Every Englishman I have met in India has approved my act, horrible as it was. What would have happened if I had not shot? I and my little force would have been swept away like chaff and then what would have happened?'[15] Montagu was concerned that the interview glossed over the facts and minimized the horrors. He released a statement on 5 May stating, 'The policy of his Majesty's Government...may be broadly stated as the employment of no more force and destruction of life than as necessary... It must regretfully and without the possibility of doubt be considered that Brigadier General Dyer's action at the Jallianwala Bagh was in complete violation of this principle...the omission to give warning before fire was opened is inexcusable. Further, Brigadier General Dyer taking no steps to see some attempt was made to give medical assistance to the dying and wounded was an omission from his obvious duty. But the gravest feature of the case against him is his avowed conception of his duty in the circumstances which confronted him...[16]

'He was not entitled to select for punishment an unarmed crowd, which, when he inflicted that punishment, had committed no act of violence, had made no attempt to oppose him by force and many members of which must have been unaware that they were disobeying his commands. The (crawling) order offended against every canon of civilised government. It is impossible to regard him as fitted to remain entrusted with the responsibilities which

---

15 Collett, Nigel, *The Butcher of Amritsar: Brigader General Reginald Dyer,* London: Hambledon Continuum, 2006, p 357.

16 Collett, Nigel, *The Butcher of Amritsar: Brigader General Reginald Dyer,* London: Hambledon Continuum, 2006, p 357.

this rank and position impose upon him. The commander in chief should be instructed to remove Brigadier General Dyer from his employment and to direct him to retire.'[17]

Dyer told the India Office he had not been given a proper opportunity to present his case. The Cabinet refused to permit him to make a representation. The Committee and Churchill wanted Dyer to be punished, but the Army Council did not agree and Dyer, whose health was failing, was permitted to resign. On 26 May, the Cabinet, based on submissions made by the Montagu committee, said:

1. Admitting the extreme gravity of the situation as it presented itself to the authorities in India generally, and to Brigadier General Dyer in particular, and appreciating the immensity of the responsibility which Brigadier General Dyer rightly felt, and recognizing the danger to the lives of Europeans and to the safety of British and Indian troops, and taking into consideration the fact that in Amritsar itself violence, murder and arson of the most savage description had occurred three days previously and the city was still practically in possession of the mob, and also that from the surrounding countryside, reports were hourly being received of similar violent outbreaks and attacks upon communications and defences in those parts, and supplemented by rumours, which there was little means of verifying and as little ground for disbelieving, fully bearing all this mind, the Secretary of State, on behalf of the Cabinet, recorded

---

17 Ibid.

the view that General Dyer was not entitled to inflict that punishment, as the mob had committed no act of violence, had made no attempt to oppose him by force, and many members of which most have been unaware that they were disobeying his commands for the purpose, in his General Dyer's own words 'of producing a sufficient moral effect from a military point of view, not only on those who were present, but more especially throughout Punjab'.

2. That the military are only entitled to use the minimum force required to disperse the crowd, and that the force actually employed was greatly in excess of that required to achieve the dispersal of the crowd, and that it resulted in lamentable and unnecessary loss of life and suffering.
3. The omission to give warning before fire was opened, was inexcusable.
4. Some steps should have been taken to see that some attempt was made to give medical assistance to the dying and the wounded.[18]

The massacre and the Punjab issue was also debated in the House of Commons on 18 July. Churchill presented the views of the Cabinet, describing the massacre as 'an episode which appears to me to be without precedent or parallel in the modern history of the British Empire… It is an extraordinary event, a monstrous event, an event which

---

18 Nair, C. Sankaran, *Autobiography of C. Sankaran Nair*, Chennai: Lady Madhavan Nair, 1966, pp 403-404.

stands in singular and sinister isolation.'[19] Churchill went on to say that Dyer had stated that he 'was confronted, by a revolutionary army'. To this statement Churchill's response was, 'What is the chief characteristic of an army? Surely it is that it is armed. This crowd was unarmed. It was not attacking anybody or anything. It was holding a seditious meeting. When fire had been opened upon it to disperse it, it tried to run away. Pinned up in a narrow place, considerably smaller than Trafalgar Square, with hardly any exits, and packed together so that one bullet would drive through three or four bodies, the people ran madly this way and the other. When the fire was directed upon the centre, they ran to the sides. The fire was directed upon the sides and they ran to the centre. Many threw themselves upon the ground, and the fire was then directed on the ground. This was continued for 8 or 10 minutes, and it stopped only when the ammunition had reached the point of exhaustion...enough ammunition being retained to provide for the safety of the force on its return journey. If more troops had been available, says this officer, the casualties would have been greater in proportion. If the road had not been so narrow, the machine guns and the armoured cars would have joined in. Finally...after 379 persons, which is about the number gathered together in this Chamber today, had been wounded, the troops at whom not even a stone had been thrown, swung round and marched away... We have to make it absolutely clear, some way or other, that this is not the British way of doing business... I do not conceal from the House my sincere, personal opinion

---

19 Ibid, p 405.

that General Dyer's conduct deserved not only the loss of employment from which so many officers are now suffering at the present time, not only the measure of censure which the Government have pronounced, but also that it should have been marked by a distinct disciplinary act, namely, his being compulsorily put upon the retired list.'[20]

The House concurred with Churchill and its members voted 247 to 37 against Dyer and in support of the Government.

Meanwhile, O'Dwyer tried to meet Montagu several times to support his actions. But he was rebuffed. He wrote, 'I spent two years in vain efforts to secure some measure of alleviation, if not for justice, for the unfortunate officers, civil and military, who had been censured or otherwise punished.'[21] Having failed to obtain any redress from Montagu, he represented the case of the civil officers verbally to Lord Reading, Lord Chelmsford's successor, before he went to India and in writing thereafter. His letter was not acknowledged. O'Dwyer continued to claim that Dyer and he had been misjudged and that the horrors they had inflicted were correct in the circumstances. In 1921, he tried to place the case before Lloyd George, the Prime Minister, through his private secretary. He was given a hearing and that was all. The Government was clear: the actions at Jallianwala Bagh and in the Punjab could not be justified.

---

20 Nair, C. Sankaran, *Autobiography of C. Sankaran Nair*, Chennai: Lady Madhavan Nair, 1966, pp 405-406.
21 O'Dwyer, Michael, *India As I Knew It*, London: Constable & Co Ltd, 1925, p 216.

THE TRIGGER

Sir Sankaran Nair had begun to feel that he could not achieve much in England as Viceroy Lord Reading was not inclined to implement further reforms even though Montagu had recommended them. He returned to India, where he could be more effective by seeking further reforms. On his return, he received an invitation to preside at a Bombay conference held to arrange a Round Table Conference with the Viceroy for the release of political prisoners and discuss remedial steps regarding the political situation in India. He accepted the offer as he wanted to ascertain whether Mahatma Gandhi truly held the will to participate in a conference to resolve these issues. When the conference was convened, he found that Gandhi was not interested; in fact, he argued that, prior to any discussions with the British government, it had to show 'penitence' in the manner India had been governed. Gandhi demanded the release of all Congress and Khilafat prisoners, the right to enrol additional volunteers for propaganda, and punishments for those mentioned in the Congress Report for the Punjab disturbances, including depriving O'Dwyer and Dyer of their pensions. Gandhi also demanded immediate grant of dominion status for India, and insisted that as per the Khilafat's demands, the French should leave Syria and the

British should leave Egypt, and that in consonance with the Indian Muslims' demand, the authority of the Caliphs of the Ottoman Empire be restored. Furthermore, he said he would only attend the conference in his personal capacity if these minimum conditions were accepted. In his opinion, the time for a conference had not arrived.

Nair felt that Gandhi's terms were impractical, and there was no point in continuing with a conference that would only have ended in a stalemate. Disillusioned, he left Bombay and accepted the post of Diwan of Indore, a princely State. As Nair expected, Gandhi's demands were rejected by the Viceroy.

While in Indore, not being a man to hold back his views, Nair wrote *Gandhi and Anarchy,* which was published in March 1922 at the Holkar State (Electric) Press. Nair, being a man of the law, did not agree with the civil disobedience movement. Further, being a "Nair", he could not accept a fight through non-violence. He did not believe that non-violence, non-cooperation and civil disobedience was the way for India to achieve Home Rule. He believed that such a movement would lead to disorder, chaos, riots and bloodshed. He raised these objections in his book as a dialogue between himself and Gandhi. He also added his criticism of the British Government's handling of the Punjab situation. He believed the Punjab disturbances took place due to the coercive methods adopted by O'Dwyer as Lieutenant Governor regarding recruitment, martial law, the bombing in Gujranwala and the condoning of Dyer's massacre at Jallianwala Bagh. In his chapter on the Punjab atrocities, he wrote, 'No one feels for the Punjab more than I do. I doubt if anyone was in a position to know more than I was. Even now, with all the enquiries made by the Hunter Commission and the Congress sub-committee many deplorable incidents as bad as any, worse perhaps, than any have not been disclosed... It is with a full knowledge of this that I make the following remarks... Before the reforms, under a Lieutenant Governor, a single individual, the atrocities in the Punjab, which we know only too well, could be committed almost with impunity.'[1] Nair implied the Punjab atrocities were committed with O'Dwyer's full knowledge and approval.

Just three copies of the book were sent to England, two of which went to the office of the Secretary of State for India in London. The third was sent to O'Dwyer by a friend of his in India.

The wily O'Dwyer, who had all but given up hope of clearing his name, saw in Nair's forcefully expressed opinions a means to salvage his tarnished reputation. He seized upon the opportunity to vindicate his actions in the face of the Hunter Commission report and the castigation his actions had received from the British Government, the Cabinet and the Parliament. He took advice from his solicitors, Sir William Joynson-Hicks and Co., and had them write to Nair in June 1922, calling his attention to the passage O'Dwyer felt was libelous and asking him to publicly withdraw the book from circulation and apologize, along with paying £1,000 to charities specified by O'Dwyer.

---

1 Nair, C. Sankaran, *Gandhi and Anarchy*, Madras: Tagore & Company, 1922, p 54; O'Dwyer, Michael, *India As I Knew It*, London: Constable & Co Ltd, 1925, p 220.

An apology would have rendered Nair's resignation from the Executive Council meaningless. Additionally, as he believed what had happened in the Punjab were atrocities, he refused to apologize or retract his statement. He was not going to be cowed down by a threat.

O'Dwyer instituted proceedings in the Court of the King's Bench in England, knowing full well that an English Court would in all likelihood side with him. Despite the Government of India, the Cabinet and the Parliament rebuking the Punjab atrocities, a large section of the English public still believed Dyer's inhuman act had saved Britain's Indian Empire – the jewel in its crown.

As this was a momentous case, on Sir Nair's request, the English courts permitted the examination on commission of witnesses in India. As far as O'Dwyer was concerned, he had no such need. Many of those he wanted to call as witnesses had already returned to England or were no longer in India. They could, thus, appear in person. These included Lord Chelmsford, Sir Munro and Major General Sir William Beynon, General Officer Commanding the Sixteenth Division in Lahore. As he felt these were strong witnesses who would undoubtedly make an impact, he asked for fewer than 10 testimonies from India.

In the summer of 1923, a commission was issued to the Chief Justice of the Punjab High Court and an Indian senior sub-judge, Rangtal, was appointed to take evidence. O'Dwyer was represented by Khan Bahadur Sheikh Abdul Qadir and Obedulla. Nair was present with his advocates Tek Chand, B.R. Puri and R.C. Soni.

Both sides were allowed to cross-examine witnesses. Voluntary follow-up examinations were also permitted. The statements were recorded in English (translated from the native language where necessary), with cross-examinations and follow-ups in question-and-answer form. These were all signed.

O'Dwyer's supporting witnesses were drawn solely from the old landed and privileged class who had not suffered from the atrocities. In addition, they had profited from the British Government's rule and were loyal to it. They were:

- Nawab Colonel Sir Malik Umar Hayat Khan Tiwana KCIE, CEI, MVO, zamindar of 48,000 bighas at Shapur, Rawalpindi, Honorary Magistrate 1st Class;
- Nawab Sir Bahram Khan Mazari, KCIE, KBE of Rojhan, Dera Ghazi Khan, jagirdar of the Mazari tribe, Member of the Punjab Legislative Council in 1919 and Member of the Council of State;
- Rai Bahadur Lala Amar Nath MBE, Kaisar-i-Hind Medallist, Sub-Registrar, Lahore, jagirdar, Secretary of the Punjab Branch of the Imperial Relief Fund Committee;
- Rai Bahadur Chowdri Lal Chand, Vakil of the High Court of Rohtak, Member of the Punjab Legislative Council Member in 1919;
- Khan Bahadur Sayyad Mehdi Shah, OBE, CIE, President of the Municipal Committee of Gojra, zamindar, Honorary Magistrate 1st Class, Honorary Civil Judge 2nd Class, lambardar, zaildar, Member of the Punjab Legislative Council in 1919;

- Honorary Major Nawab Sir Chad Baksh OBE, KCIE, Vice President of the Council of Regency, Bahawalpur State;
- Honorary Major Nawab Sir Khuda Baksh Tiwana OBE, KCIE, Vice President of the Council of Regency, Bahawalpur State.

Nair's witnesses could not have been more different. Apart from Sir Muhammed Shafi of Lahore, a member of the Government of India; Sir Setalvad, a member of the Hunter Commission; Home Secretary for the Government of India Raja Narendra Nath; and Raizada Bhagat Ram, formerly of the Punjab Legislative Council, his witnesses were men of relatively low status and included 15 lawyers, 11 medical men (doctors, surgeons and a dentist), three educators (professors or teachers) and a few businessmen. A very large number of people's testimonies were documented.

Once the evidence was procured, the stage was set for the trial with both parties engaging leading barristers to represent them. O'Dwyer was represented by Ernest Charles KC and Sir Hugh Fraser. Nair entrusted his case to Sir Patrick Hastings, one of the most prominent barristers in England at the time. Hastings had first risen to prominence as a result of the Case of the Hooded Man in 1912, and became noted for his cross-examination skills. After his success in *Gruban v Booth* in 1917, his practice had steadily grown and, in 1919, he had become a King's Counsel (KC).

But Sir Patrick Hastings was elevated to Attorney General once the new Labour government came into power before the case came up, and could not appear for Nair. He then entrusted the case to Sir John Simon, another eminent barrister.

Simon went through all the papers and evidence and opined that the case was damaging to O'Dwyer. He said that if all that happened in Punjab was published in England there would be a furore. However, the day before the trial was due to take place, Nair received a telegram from Simon, who was in Paris, expressing his inability to conduct the case. His abrupt withdrawal left Nair without a lawyer on the eve of the trial.

Caught in a difficult predicament, Nair was forced to engage Sir Walter Schwabe, a former Chief Justice of the Madras High Court. Schwabe, sensing an opportunity, readily accepted the case if he was given the same fee as Sir Simon, even though he was certainly not of the same calibre as Simon or Hastings. To make matters worse, Schwabe did not even have adequate time to prepare for the case. Hubert J. Wallington KC and J.M. Parish assisted him.

It is unclear as to why Nair did not choose to defend himself when Simon withdrew. He would have certainly acquitted himself better than Schwabe who was not as experienced, strong or as knowledgeable about the case. Nonetheless, his decision to fight an Englishman in an English court was a courageous move. There were innumerable disadvantages for Nair, not least of which was a less-than-proficient legal practitioner. The trial was to be held in England, the jury would be English, and because the witnesses providing evidence for the defence could not be present, their evidence would merely be read out, leaving it open to possible misinterpretation. Most significant of all was the fact that the English continued to believe themselves to be far superior to Indians, which is why the latter were rarely treated fairly. English juries had acquitted Englishmen who had killed Indians (one was acquitted after killing a coolie and another after killing a washerman who had asked for his wages) and here was an Indian accusing an Englishman of atrocities, in an English court. It was destined to be a case that made history.

THE TRIAL

On the morning of 30 April 1924, Sir Sankaran Nair stepped out of the comfortable four-poster bed in the large five-bedroom Georgian house he had rented for the duration of the case. He usually resided at the National Liberal Club at Whitehall in central London, but as his wife and family had joined him, he had opted for a well-furnished and comfortable home that was not too far from the Court of King's Bench. Although he was an early riser, waking up at 4.30 a.m. on most days, he couldn't get any sleep the previous night with his brain swarming with thoughts about the case. Finally, at 4 a.m., he gave up all attempts to sleep.

The only thing he was certain of was that fighting this case was the right thing to do. He felt he had to make every attempt to ensure that a massacre like Jallianwala Bagh never happened again. But would fighting a case of libel actually ensure this? Or would he end up making a fool of himself, with India none the better for it at the end? He had been quite certain of his decision to fight O'Dwyer, yet he was now besieged with demoralizing thoughts. He saw his wife sleeping comfortably in the featherdown bed, and he was grateful she remained undisturbed by all the turbulence in his life.

He quietly slipped out of the room and headed to the ground floor study, the room in which he felt most at ease. The oak-panelled room was dominated by a heavy mahogany writing desk with a swivel leather upholstered chair that neatly fitted under it. A small thermos of tea that his wife had left for him knowing his penchant for an early morning 'cuppa' was on the desk. Maids willing to work from the crack of dawn were hard to come by in London. When he had rented an apartment while still a member of the Secretary of State's Council, his wife had hired an elderly Quaker woman who qualified for the position as she neither smoked nor drank and, most importantly, was not averse to waking at the unearthly hour of 4.30 a.m. The day after she was hired, she efficiently brought the tea to his bedroom, only to be horrified at the sight of a huge six-foot-tall, half-naked man standing on his head in the middle of the room. Startled out of her wits, she dropped the tray and ran out of the house as fast as she could, and was never heard from again. Sir Nair, unruffled, continued with his *sirshasan*. Word of the poor maid's predicament must have spread far and wide, and therefore the Nairs always had difficulty finding good help after that incident.

Nair now poured some tea into the Royal Doulton china cup placed alongside the thermos and eased himself into the chair. His eyes drifted to the collection of leather-bound first editions that were cramped into ornate book cases. Perhaps he would have time in the coming weeks to relax and catch up on some reading, he thought idly.

Nair wanted to arrive early to court on the first day of the trial. His son, Ramunni Menon Palat, would bring his wife and daughters later. His son-in-law, Madhavan Nair (later a privy councilor himself), would accompany him to court. Nair would have preferred to walk the short distance but the cold and wet morning played spoilsport. The April of 1924 had seen some of the heaviest rainfall in years. The sun had made tentative attempts to shine for a few days, but with little success. Sir Nair plucked his warm, woollen coat and top hat off the hat rack. Pulling his collar up and tying a scarf around his neck, he stepped into the cab that Madhavan had hailed for him.

It took them a few minutes to reach the courthouse. When Sir Nair walked inside the magnificent Gothic building he saw that his counsels Schwabe and Wallington KC were already seated at the head of the courtroom. He sat down in the vacant seat next to them. On the other side sat O'Dwyer's counsel, Ernest Charles KC and Hugh Fraser, poring over their notes. O'Dwyer was outside the courtroom, shaking hands and conversing with his supporters.

As the time for the hearing got closer, a surge of people crowded into the courtroom. The defendant's sympathizers sat behind his counsel. Soon, there was hardly any space left for outsiders in the courtroom. Nair turned around and smiled at his wife and daughters, who looked anxious. This was the first time they had been to a court in England and they were understandably nervous. His son, a barrister himself, was seated behind him.

The trial went on for five-and-a-half weeks – the longest civil case at that time – and from the very first day, the courtroom was crowded, with people continuing to pour was to prove what had occurred in Amritsar on 13 April 1919 was an atrocity and that O'Dwyer was complicit in the massacre. McCardie countered this by asking him if Dyer's actions were to 'preserve the Punjab', would Schwabe still say 'it was not necessary'?[2]

By cleverly steering the subject away from the subject of the trial – the onus on O'Dwyer for the Punjab massacre – towards Dyer and the morality of his actions, even though Dyer's actions and guilt were completely irrelevant to this trial, McCardie was clearly defending the case for O'Dwyer. Schwabe, a little nonplussed, asked the judge to give him a chance to present his case. He added that the matters to be placed before the court were grave and that he would prove what was done in Amritsar 'was an atrocity from any point of view'.[3]

Nair was surprised at McCardie's interjections. As a judge himself, he knew McCardie's role was to ensure a fair trial and not state opinions that may influence the jury. However, on the very first day of the trial, the judge had already begun to voice his strong opinions.

Following the opening statements, the prosecution began to argue their case. The first witness the defence called to the stand was O'Dwyer himself. The prosecution took the next 15-and-a-half days to put forth their case, the first six of which were spent questioning O'Dwyer.

O'Dwyer strode to the witness box looking indignant, outraged and hurt. Charles began the examination by asking

---

[2] Nair, C. Sankaran, *Autobiography of C. Sankaran Nair*, Chennai: Lady Madhavan Nair, 1966, p 414.
[3] Ibid.

the perils the English bore to protect the Empire. Indians, of course, were portrayed as rebels, extremists and seditionists.

The leading counsel for Nair, Sir Walter Schwabe, had recently returned to England after having served as Chief Justice of the Madras High Court for three years. He was of a scholarly disposition and had written several books. But, while he was extremely knowledgeable, he was not a trial lawyer.

After Charles completed his opening remarks, Schwabe, a heavy-built man, rose slowly, addressed the judge with respect, and explained to the jury that there was no case for defamation as the comments made in the book were factually correct. He went on to say he would, during the course of the trial, prove that as Lieutenant Governor of the Punjab, O'Dwyer had caused atrocities to be committed.

Normally, after the plaintiff and the defence have made their opening statements, the defence calls its first witness. However, this did not happen. As soon as Schwabe had completed his opening address, Justice McCardie asked Schwabe whether he intended to prove General Dyer was right or wrong. Schwabe told him that that was not the intent. At this juncture, McCardie pointed out to the jury that a person may be forced to take action that may appear to be repellent later when the safety of the Indian Empire and the wider Empire was concerned in order to protect British interests.

He, therefore, demanded to know from Schwabe what indeed he proposed to raise.

Schwabe was taken aback by the nature of McCardie's remark. He quietly and calmly told the judge that his intent public interest. He pleaded that, on 13 April 1919, Dyer had committed an atrocity by ordering the shooting of innocent persons at Jallianwala Bagh, and that O'Dwyer, as the then Lieutenant Governor General of Punjab and the final authority, caused or was responsible for the commission of the said atrocity.

After the jury had been sworn in, O'Dwyer's lawyer Ernest B. Charles strode to the middle of the courtroom and addressed the jury for the next two-and-a-half hours. Charles described O'Dwyer as a paragon of men, a provincial governor who had averted a mutiny. He extolled him for his services during the war, mentioning his procurement of money, men and food for the Imperial Army. In an aggrieved tone, while looking accusingly at Nair, he said that O'Dwyer's acts that had saved the Empire were now being defamed as atrocities and that O'Dwyer was here to clear his name. With regard to the Jallianwala Bagh massacre, he said, 'I am not here to deal with the matter as to what General Dyer did.' But he went onto do just that. 'Some people consider what General Dyer did was right and some people think that he went too far... In the present case, knowing what happened on the 10th, having proclaimed that there should be no meeting, knowing that there should be no meeting, knowing they were full of murder and seditions, General Dyer did what he conceived to be his duty at any rate.'[1]

Charles' words were clearly meant to kindle the sympathy of the English jury for their own people. He exaggerated

---

1   Nair, C. Sankaran, *Autobiography of C. Sankaran Nair*, Chennai: Lady Madhavan Nair, 1966, p 413.

in, including several eminent dignitaries. On one occasion, the Maharaja of Bikaner came to hear the proceedings. Not one to be left standing or sitting amongst the hoi-polloi, he sat alongside the judge on the dais.

At precisely 10 a.m., the court clerk cried out, 'All rise,' and the presiding judge, Justice Henry McCardie, strode in. McCardie was clean shaven with bushy eyebrows, piercing eyes and thin lips. Though of medium height and a stocky build, he gave the impression of being taller than he actually was with his athletic gait. Nair observed that the judge walked with his feet turned outward.

The all-English jury comprised nine men and three women. One of them, a Jewish man, took his oath without placing his hand on the Bible. They were middle-class men and women of varying ages grappling with court procedures and, for the most part, out of their depth. They seemed to be unfamiliar with India, Indians or any Indian terminology.

McCardie was an opinionated judge. *The Sunday Express* in December 1931 would write that he would be remembered as a judicial infidel and a rogue judge running amok, likening him to a bull in a china shop. He had his own opinion on the matters he tried and did not hesitate to plague the counsel if he was not in agreement. Unlike most judges, he unambiguously made his views known to the jury. Hence, O'Dwyer was at a distinct advantage. McCardie had come to the trial with fixed ideas about the violence in Punjab that were similar to those of O'Dwyer.

Nair had pleaded justification in support of the statement he had made in *Gandhi and Anarchy* and also raised the plea of fair and bonafide (good faith) comment on a matter of

O'Dwyer about his career in India, making sure he came across as an outstanding official. The judge and jury were very impressed by O'Dwyer's statement that he governed a country twice as large as England with a population of 21 million – a man the British should be extremely proud of for his contributions to the Empire and for averting a mutiny by taking bold steps.

After O'Dwyer deposed, Schwabe cross-examined him. Schwabe had made his case with a strong opening speech and his cross-examination of O'Dwyer was equally forceful. O'Dwyer now lost some of his bluster and grew nervous. His constant movements in the jury box betrayed his anxiety. Clearly, the man was uncomfortable on being questioned. On being presented with Dyer's statements before the Hunter Commission, O'Dwyer had to admit that he was not prepared to justify Dyer's conduct if Dyer had indeed told the Hunter Committee that he had decided to fire as soon as he had arrived without giving the crowd an opportunity to disperse and continued to fire, finally leaving without a care for the wounded.

As the questioning continued, O'Dwyer grew highly excitable with his responses and, at one point, he got so out of breath that his counsel needed to step in to request a recess. There were also moments when the judge, realizing O'Dwyer's predicament, interjected with his comments and clarifications. Over the next few days, Schwabe continued to ask O'Dwyer whether Dyer's decision to fire on the crowd, with the aim of causing widespread fear throughout the Punjab, was justified. O'Dwyer, knowing he was losing ground, evaded the question by saying it was not fair for him to comment on a military act. Yet, to diffuse to some extent the brutality of Dyer's actions, he said Dyer had probably acted as such because he was faced with a bludgeon army.[4]

However, O'Dwyer accepted no responsibility for Dyer's appointment. He said Dyer had not been sent by him to the Punjab but by his commanding general to restore order there.

Realizing that Schwabe's line of questioning was slowly taking the shine off the glowing presentation of O'Dwyer over the first few days, Justice McCardie decided to step in to bolster the plaintiff's case. With absolutely no basis or evidence to support his statements, the judge said anyone with the slightest imagination could depict the situation at Amritsar. Explaining further, again with no evidence, he added that the police had completely lost control. Perhaps for the first time at a trial hearing, imagination was being given credence over facts. The judge almost chastised Schwabe when he stated that the defence counsel seemed to ignore the grave consequences that might have followed had Dyer's force been destroyed. Just in case the 'consequences' were not apparent to the jury, McCardie suggested that, had Dyer's forces been destroyed, Amritsar would have been delivered to the mob. The judge then even went on to warn Schwabe that the questions he was raising would end up hampering those dealing with threats of anarchy in the future.

O'Dwyer, chuffed with the support he was receiving, concluded by saying that the highest military authorities in

---

4 'O'Dwyer – Nair Libel Suit: Gen Dyer's Deeds, Moral Effect Theory', *The Hindu*, 5 May 1924.

India and England had approved Dyer's actions. However, knowing this was not true, Schwabe was quick to refute it and point out that the Secretary of State for India, the Government of India and the Army Council had all denounced Dyer's actions. O'Dwyer opined, however, that Dyer had been condemned not on merit but on political expediency. McCardie concurred strongly and, even though he was not a military man and had never been to India, stated that relieving Dyer of his position was an error.

In the days that followed, the judge often intervened to portray for the jury imaginary scenarios that suggested appalling consequences if Dyer's troops had been surrounded by the 'bludgeon army' and destroyed, making it seem as though Dyer had been faced with an army whereas the truth was he was facing a group of unarmed men, women and children, most of whom were there to celebrate a festival.

O'Dwyer, desperate to disassociate himself from the atrocities, repudiated that the general instructions he gave to Commissioner Kitchin had led to the Amritsar massacre. Playing the aggrieved victim to the hilt, he complained bitterly about the Hunter Committee, where he said he was treated as a criminal without being given adequate opportunity to defend himself. However, Schwabe did not let up. He countered that the shooting by Dyer was an atrocity committed under O'Dwyer's general direction. He argued O'Dwyer had sufficient knowledge of the situation and had given his consent by putting Dyer in charge. Though he admitted to accepting the appointment of Dyer after his arrival at Amritsar, O'Dwyer clarified he had not met Dyer prior to the Jallianwala incident but only knew of his reputation as a distinguished officer with a fine record. O'Dwyer also stressed that he had no control over the military when the city was under martial law. He claimed he, too, had to live under martial law and on one occasion he himself had not been permitted to travel to Amritsar.

As for the Gujranwala bombing, O'Dwyer had to acknowledge that the aircraft had been sent on his orders, but only because there was no time to send military reinforcements. He was asked whether he thought bombing and machine-gunning innocent people two miles away from Gujranwala, who were either travelling out of or going towards the town, could be justified. O'Dwyer said they could have been going to Gujranwala to join in the disturbances. He shrugged off responsibility for the bombings, saying they had been carried out on the basis of the assessments of English officers who thought the bombings were justifiable as the townspeople were creating disturbances, though there was no evidence of this.

McCardie once again strengthened the plaintiff's plea by addressing the jury and stating that the question was whether one would be entitled to kill hundreds to prevent the death of half a million. In response, Schwabe, now not just to the plaintiff and the jury but also to the judge, stated that using machine guns on people from an aircraft was an atrocity, and the fact remained that the aviators had indiscriminately shot innocent people even as O'Dwyer claimed he had told the aviators to be careful.

McCardie opined that the question was only of application and not one of principle. He said that when it was necessary to suppress crime and anarchy, he saw no difference between the baton stick of a policeman, the rifle of a soldier and the use of a machine gun from an aircraft. In short, he saw nothing wrong in mowing down innocents who had not engaged in any violent acts. Several patriotic Englishmen on the jury nodded sagaciously in response to this statement.

The case moved on to questions about the Lahore arrests. O'Dwyer stoutly denied that action had been taken against political opponents. He instead claimed that those arrested were implicated in a widespread rebellion and incitements to mutiny, but he could provide no actual evidence to back his claim. However, he was compelled to agree that they should not have been incarcerated for as long as they had been.

When the matter of the flogging orders was brought up, O'Dwyer said he could not condemn the order as he was not made aware of it, adding that the person responsible, S.M. Jacob, the Director of Agriculture, had been censured. Schwabe declared that the manner of the flogging was an outrage. But as was turning out to be the norm, the judge intervened once again to say these measures were not excessive and he felt that there was no need for Montagu to censure Jacob. He added that under martial law Jacob was allowed to whip those guilty of crimes. O'Dwyer then added that the floggings had been carried out with a cane, which was milder than a whip. He even suggested that the people had asked to be flogged as opposed to being fined. When questioned about the whipping of schoolboys at Kasur, O'Dwyer claimed the whole school had been implicated in disturbances. Schwabe then asked if O'Dwyer felt the order compelling students to walk 17 miles in the hot Lahore sun for roll calls and to report to the military officer was fair. O'Dwyer once again said that many of the students were rebels and these disciplinary measures were necessary to keep them out of mischief. Schwabe pointed out there had been children as young as six in the group. O'Dwyer then conveniently refused to accept responsibility for Colonel Johnson's (the Martial Law Administrator in Lahore) acts.

As far as the order for salaaming, O'Dwyer agreed that Indians of position had resented it. He relented and said that he, too, felt it to be injudicious.

At the end of six days, O'Dwyer's testimony concluded. Despite protests by Schwabe, McCardie once again told the jury that General Dyer and others who had been censured had not been represented by counsel at the Hunter Committee hearings, and the censure orders did not fully consider all the facts.

Subsequent to O'Dwyer's deposition, the aforementioned witnesses were called on his behalf.

However, Dyer was not called as his testimony at the Hunter Committee had resulted in censure from the Government of India, the Cabinet and Parliament, and this would have weakened Dyer's deposition. O'Dwyer's counsel, Charles, cleverly played on Dyer's illness and hence his inability to depose. The fact was that, though ill, Dyer was not exactly at death's door as portrayed by Charles, and died three years later. But McCardie made his views clear by saying he wanted to make sure a dying man got a fair hearing from a living jury, reiterating his opinion that Dyer had not got a fair hearing from the Hunter Commission.

Lord Chelmsford was the plaintiff's first witness. As Viceroy, he had initially supported the actions of Dyer and O'Dwyer. After the Hunter Committee report, however, he had switched his views and supported the Hunter Committee's findings. As the First Lord of the Admiralty at the time of the trial, he was careful not to go against either the Government or his own dispatches. He said that martial law had been imposed at the request of O'Dwyer and that the General Officer Commanding was instructed to act in consultation with the Lieutenant Governor, which made O'Dwyer *de facto* if not *de jure* responsible.[5] He also stated that if O'Dwyer had brought to the notice of the Government of India any case in which military authorities had disregarded his advice, the Government would have taken serious action against that person, suggesting that every atrocity under martial law had O'Dwyer's tacit approval. Chelmsford said he was horrified with the crawling order, and claimed he had nothing to do with the instruction that troops should fire on people to make an example of them. When asked about Sir Nair's resignation, he said Nair had been disturbed by the administration of martial law and by barristers not being permitted to enter the Punjab to defend those incarcerated.

Chelmsford's deposition did little to strengthen O'Dwyer's case. Much of the evidence merely cleared him of all blame for the atrocities and implicated O'Dwyer.

---

5   O'Dwyer, Michael, *India As I Knew It*, London: Constable & Co Ltd, 1925, p 216.

McCardie refrained from commenting or refuting Chelmsford, perhaps because the judge was awed by the presence of the First Lord of the Admiralty in his court.

Major General Sir William Beynon appeared for O'Dwyer next. He was an old campaigner and had served in every frontier war since 1887. As expected, he defended Dyer's actions at Jallianwala Bagh, even stating that Dyer's statements to the Hunter Committee (he had given three different statements) were not reliable and that he strongly believed Dyer's original statement, which was that he had opened fire as the crowd was surging and because he feared for the safety of his troops. He even opined that the evidence Dyer gave the Hunter Commission was wrong. When it was pointed out that Dyer had not changed his story even to the Army Council, Beynon stoutly refused to accept this and suggested Dyer had suffered so enormously that he had forgotten the sequence of events.

The next witness, A.J.W. Kitchin, had been the Commissioner of the Lahore Division at the time, and was thus superior to Amritsar Deputy Commissioner Miles Irving. Kitchin had been censured by the Government after the Hunter Committee report for handing over control of Amritsar to the military without giving them clear instructions. Kitchin had strongly supported Dyer's actions. In his deposition, he said O'Dwyer had asked him to go to Amritsar on 14 April to ensure there would be no firing. But when he met Dyer, the latter told him about the shooting saying he had done his horrible duty and that it had been the right thing to do. Kitchin went so far as to comment that Dyer had acted because of the unreliability and untrustworthiness of Indian soldiers.

The defence, in response, brought to attention the point that Lieutenant General Sir Havelock Hudson, Adjutant-General in India, had dismissed any suggestions that the Indian Army had become unreliable. Their efforts during the First World War had been highly appreciated. Had Indian troops been unreliable, it was unlikely the British would have been so hell-bent on recruiting Indians. Even Dyer would refute such allegations, as he had an excellent rapport with Indian soldiers.

When Max Leigh, Assistant Commissioner at Shahpur deposed, he refuted the charge that officials had accepted recruits for the army. He also denied that he had instructed harsher treatment of landowners who did not get recruits and all other compulsive tactics used on locals. On cross-examination, however, he admitted that in one case 75 men had been released from jail and recruited to the army. He did not say whether this was a coincidence or whether more could be read into this convenient transaction.

Basil Gibson, the Commissioner at Shahpur, concurred with Leigh and claimed that recruitment was voluntary and he had not received any complaint about it. Although he said there had been a report that deserters were made to sit on thistles, he admitted the matter had not been investigated because the official entrusted with the investigation had been arrested. The reason for the arrest, of course, remained a mystery.

The first Indian to appear in person in support of O'Dwyer was the Honorable Nawab Sir Muhamad Akbar Khan, recruiting officer and Chief of Hoti in Peshawar, and former Second-in-Command 129th Baluchis. He was in charge of a divisional recruiting station in 1917. Scion of a wealthy and influential family, he had acted as an aide de camp to George V. On being questioned, he said he had not heard of any coercion during recruitment.

Then Lieutenant Colonel Frank Johnson was called to the stand. He maintained that the mob had been in possession of Amritsar from 10 April onwards and Dyer had taken the necessary actions to retake control of the city. Colonel North, Commandant of the Fort in Amritsar, said a large crowd was cutting down trees and issuing calls to 'kill the white people'.[6] He claimed the mob was armed with small axes. North said he had been trapped inside the fort for several days and he had to remain there as the reserve rifles and a very large sum in gold coins had to be safeguarded.

Captain John T. Botting of the Royal Field Artillery, too, had been in Amritsar and had not given evidence to the Hunter Committee. Botting now told the court he had been commanding British and Indian troops of the 12th Ammunition Column in Amritsar as part of the city's permanent garrison that comprised 8 white and 200 Indian soldiers. Botting refuted Kitchin's view on Indian soldiers and said that they were totally loyal. He told the court he had sent a few Indian soldiers in native dress to mix with the crowds to find out what was happening on the day. Their report suggested that the British Government was no longer ruling and that the people were defiant, and after Dyer's shooting, the situation changed completely. People began to smile and

---

6 O'Dwyer, Michael, *India As I Knew It*, London: Constable & Co Ltd, 1925, p 232.

shops reopened. Botting believed that but for Dyer's action, trouble would have been worse, although one could refute his arguments because an environment of fear and terror had spread across the Punjab after the massacre. It would be hard to imagine that a people who had just lost near and dear ones in an unexpected, horrific encounter would be joyous and capable of carrying on their everyday affairs as if nothing had happened.

The next witness was Sir Patrick Eagan, who had been Financial Controller in the Punjab. He said that gross misrepresentations of the Rowlatt Act had preceded the disturbances and believed that the primary object of the conspiracy in Punjab was not to overthrow the British Government but to appeal to the Government to withdraw the Act and extort political concessions.

General Sir George Carmichael Munro's testimony was presented on oath from abroad as he was the Governor of Gibraltar at the time of the trial. As Commander-in-Chief in India, he had been instrumental in dismissing Dyer from his post, upset by the admission of his intention to fire without warning, and asking him to return to England without any formal disciplinary action. Munro had been much criticized for this within the Army and in India. In his evidence to the court, he revealed yet another cause to be upset with Dyer. Dyer had lied to him regarding the infamous crawling order. Munro said that as soon as he heard of it, he sent an order to Dyer to withdraw the order. Dyer had replied saying the order had been cancelled as soon as he had heard of it even before Munro's telegram arrived, withholding the fact that it was he who had initiated the order. Though his testimony was a scathing attack on Dyer, Munro gave O'Dwyer a clean chit. Regarding O'Dwyer's proclamation of martial law in the Punjab, Munro felt the situation required its imposition. He stressed that O'Dwyer was not responsible for any irregularities under martial law.

Besides the Honourable Nawab Sir Muhamad Akbar Khan, O'Dwyer also had other Indian witnesses give their evidence on his behalf in India. All of them gave glowing reports of his governorship of the Punjab. However, on cross examination, most of them admitted there had been cases where men were forcibly recruited into the army.

O'Dwyer and the majority of witnesses who deposed for him lauded the actions of Dyer. Curiously, however, no one acknowledged Dyer's appointment to the Punjab. While O'Dwyer said Dyer had been sent to the Punjab by his Commanding Officer, Major General Beynon, the latter testified that he had, in fact, sent Lieutenant Colonel Morgan to take charge and not Dyer. Dyer had taken command as he was the seniormost officer in Amritsar.

After the plaintiff presented his witnesses, Schwabe took the floor and vigorously denounced O'Dwyer's mentality, policy and methods. He described O'Dwyer as a man with hard and unbending views, brooking no interference and ready to raise controversy on the slightest occasion. Schwabe said that in the first week of the trial, O'Dwyer had attempted to suggest his was the official view, relegating the view and conclusions made by the Government of India, the Hunter Committee and the Cabinet to be unofficial. O'Dwyer as administrative head of the Punjab had to bear the responsibility of what had occurred in the state, he argued. After five years of the incidents, sitting in faraway England, O'Dwyer, Schwabe said, was asking the jury to believe the conclusions arrived at after such a thorough, detailed investigation by the Government were wrong. Further, Schwabe pointed out that O'Dwyer was quick to use evidence from the Hunter Committee when it suited him. When it did not, he conveniently blamed Indian shorthand writers or said that he did not get a fair hearing before the Commission.

Schwabe pointed out that widespread conspiracy against the Government and suspected disloyalty of Indian troops had been put forward as an excuse for the happenings at Lahore and Amritsar in April 1919 without any evidence. Even if true, he argued, there was no justification for the gruesome cruelties perpetrated. The Punjab was absolutely 'dragooned'[7]. Politicians were treated as criminals 'of the deepest dye'[8]. The bombing at Gujranwala was indefensible. O'Dwyer's policy was to strike terror in the Punjab and produce a moral effect.

Similarly, the recruitment methods adopted in 1918 were terrorism in the worst form and as despicable as could be conceived, Schwabe argued. While he clarified that O'Dwyer himself did not exercise terrorism, but terrorism of the worst form had occurred under his government. From place after place had emerged reports of the most disgraceful campaign of terror and O'Dwyer had taken no steps to stop them.

---

7 'The Defence Case: Counsel's Argument', *The Hindu*, 21 May 1924.
8 Ibid.

Schwabe said the evidence had shown the plaintiff was officially and personally responsible for the Punjab atrocities, citing the fact that it was at O'Dwyer's insistence that a senior officer had been sent to Amritsar, and the day after the massacre, he had by telegram conveyed his approval of Dyer's action. In addition, as Chelmsford had pointed out, martial law was to be administered with the advice and approval of O'Dwyer. Furthermore, Schwabe stated that the defence did not accept the view that Dyer's actions had saved the situation and averted a rebel mutiny of the same scale as in 1857.

Schwabe brought to attention the fact that Sir Nair regarded the administration of justice in England as one of the greatest things in the world and his belief that he would get a fair trial before an English jury was the reason he had agreed to defend himself in England before an English judge and jury. Perhaps the defence counsel hoped to nudge McCardie into conducting a fair and impartial hearing.

Sir Schwabe submitted that, after hearing his evidence, the jury would conclude the defendant was justified in his comments that were fair and in public interest. It was then time for him to present witness statements. Unlike O'Dwyer's witnesses, Sir Nair's witnesses were not eminent personages but of a lower status. These included lawyers, businessmen, doctors and educators. As they could not travel to England for the trial, their evidence had been taken on commission in India. Since there were several hundred depositions, McCardie limited the number of depositions that could be presented as evidence to 125. Only two witnesses appeared in person for the defence –

Gerald Wathen, who in 1919 was the Principal of the Khalsa College, and Sir Harkisen Lal, a former Minister of the Punjab Government and who had been imprisoned under the martial order. Lal had come to England on his own expense to give evidence.

After Schwabe's opening address, the evidence taken on commission were read out. It must be mentioned that reading out evidence in court can neither capture the attention of the audience nor reflect the emotions of the witness adequately. To make matters worse, McCardie made it plain that he gave far less importance to these oral dispositions compared to the evidence of the English generals, officers and functionaries who had appeared before the jury.

Of the 125 depositions, 68 related to the coerced recruitment of soldiers, 17 to the imposition of martial law, 8 to the events leading up to Jallianwala Bagh and 15 to the massacre and other incidents in its aftermath, such as the aerial bombing of Gujranwala, floggings and incarcerations.

All witnesses deposing against recruitment complained of being penalized by various officials if they failed to influence men to join the army or declined to enlist themselves. One witness said that certain villages were subjected to night raids by armed forces in which youth and children were taken from their beds and forced to enlist. The depositions spoke of torture inflicted on both men and women, such as the bramble-and-thornbush treatment, the durbars held for recruitments, the wholesale declaration of individuals to be members of a criminal tribe and having their titles taken away, and the misuse of the judicial process by which recruitment was offered as an alternative to imprisonment.

Witnesses recounted how bribes were paid to allow recruiters to fill their quotas. Several depositions described the public flogging in Amritsar.

The evidence was personal, compelling and horrifying. In some villages, young men hid from the sight of the recruiters and those who were caught were stripped naked, beaten with sticks and had brambles placed between their legs. Others were handcuffed and made to sit on thorns in the sun, bent double while holding their ears through their legs. In court, at Sir Schwabe's request, Sir Nair demonstrated how this was done for the benefit of the jurors. These revelations caused a sensation in the court.

Witnesses testified that men were deprived even of loin clothes and women were compelled to pull strings tied to men's private parts. There were several acts recorded against women who were made to remove their veils and harassed to provide false testimony. Three staff members of the King Edward College in Lahore stated that their students were made to march two miles twice a day to the Punjab Club and back after the imposition of martial law to give attendance. The Principal of Sanathan Dharm College said his students were arrested and held at the fort for removing martial law posters. In Dyal Singh College, students were subjected to compulsory roll call four times a day. Others testified they were arrested without cause and incarcerated in filthy conditions without any explanation for long periods of time. A schoolboy testified that, to identify persons who had not adhered to martial law regulations, identity parades had been held, and when no one could be identified, three children from each school had been selected and flogged.

Other witnesses described similar roll calls at Sangla, the imposition of martial law at Lyallpur and the outbreak of violence followed by the aerial bombing at Gujranwala, about which graphic evidence was also given. The testimonies of those who were deposed about the events in Amritsar in the days before the Jallianwala Bagh massacre included those of Dr Satya Pal, who was charged with several crimes despite no evidence against him and was sentenced to life in a prison colony in the Andamans without being given an opportunity to defend himself. Fifteen people spoke about the massacre in Jallianwala Bagh, 11 of them clearly stating they were unaware of Dyer's proclamation against public meetings. Others said the soldiers had fired as soon as they arrived, continuing to shoot people in the back even as they were fleeing. Other depositions cast light on the events after the shooting, including those of doctors who said Colonel Smith did not permit the wounded to be treated in hospitals and when they tried to intervene, threatened them with flogging. Colonel Smith is also said to have stated that for every European, a thousand Indians would be killed.

Gerald Ansruther Wathen, former Principal of Khalsa College in Amritsar, who had returned to England and was now the headmaster of a school, was present in court to testify on behalf of Sir Nair. A quiet, disciplined man, he said there had been no noticeable unrest among students, but there had been growing distress against the Rowlatt Act in Amritsar. After the murder of Europeans, he arranged for older students to form themselves into companies of special constables to ascertain the mood of the people. On the day before the massacre, a young English subaltern had ridden into the grounds of the college, firing his gun and shouting in Hindi, 'Where is the Sahib?' The officer had brought Wathen a message from Dyer requiring him to go to the military club. Wathen had refused, saying he preferred to stay in the college with his students. A while later, a military escort was sent requiring his presence.[9] He was thus compelled to move to the club and remained there during the massacre as Dyer had wanted all Englishmen to remain under military protection.

After the shooting, Wathen had a conversation with Dyer and later left with another Englishman for Lahore, with a written message for O'Dwyer. He conveyed the report on the Jallianwala shooting to O'Dwyer the same night and urged him to go to Amritsar and take charge. Wathen thought Dyer had made a mistake in not warning the people at the Bagh. On cross-examination, he opined that a little firing may have been justified provided notice had been given.

When Wathen returned to Amritsar the next day, he found the students frightened. Contradicting Captain John T. Botting, who had testified that locals were smiling and going about their day-to-day business the day after the massacre, Wathen said there were no smiling faces and that killing so many people was a mistake. He rode on horseback through the bazaars and was treated with reverence out of fear because he was an Englishman, which he did not appreciate. He suggested Sikh women would never forgive or forget what had happened at Amritsar and that it was the women more than the men who had resented the shooting

---

9 'More Evidence: Recruiting Scandals', *The Hindu*, 23 May 1924.

and the humiliating orders subsequently issued by British authorities.

Nair's other witness in court was Lala Harkishen Lal, a prominent industrialist and politician. Lal had been a member of the Punjab Government and was associated with several newspapers. Lal had been a director of the *Bande Mataram* newspaper, but he clarified in court that he had no hand in what the paper published. He had severed his ties with it after becoming a minister. A commanding figure with a drooping white moustache and turbaned head, Lal described the public antipathy against the Rowlatt Act. He said that conditions in Lahore between 8-12 April were normal and detailed his efforts with lawyer and nationalist Lala Dunichand and others to bring the strike to an end. He said he was against revolutionary and seditious movements and that he had done everything he could to help the Government and pacify the people.

Lal said he had come to know of the 10 April firings in Lahore only when he and others were asked to see the Deputy Commissioner the next day. The Deputy Commissioner had asked them to question people and ascertain their feelings, which they were unable to until the corpses were given back to the families. The bodies were not given back and though Lal and others did their utmost to have shops reopened, they were unsuccessful. The general feeling among the public was that they were being treated cruelly and wanted assurance this would not happen again. There had been no talk of abolishing British rule, he maintained. At a town hall meeting on 13 April, several representatives told the Deputy Commissioner that unless there was an assurance that things would improve and troops were withdrawn, it would be difficult to get the people to open their shops. The Deputy Commissioner said this was unlikely and that martial law would be proclaimed.

Lal stated that, on 14 April, he was ordered by a police official to sign a document under the Defence of India Act to deport himself to another state. He was detained with others till 6 May, when he was jailed on receipt of a telegram from O'Dwyer. He was then charged with waging war against the king and was convicted by court martial on 5 July and sentenced to life in prison with forfeiture of his property. This was despite him helping the Government, he said. Lal was later released under general amnesty on 23 December 1919.

Sir Nair began his testimony once Lal finished, nearly a month after the hearings began. Unlike O'Dwyer, Nair was comfortable in the courtroom, an arena with which he was familiar. He remained unruffled and composed through his entire deposition and cross-examination, both by the counsel for the plaintiff and the judge. Nair said he did not agree with O'Dwyer's methods of administration in the Punjab and that men from other parts had often complained to him about it. Nair had agreed to the proclamation of martial law in Amritsar and Lahore because he believed it would restore peace, law and order. He was not, however, consulted on the proclamation of martial law in Lyallpur, Gujrat and Gujranwala. While he was in Simla, he had received complaints about floggings, the use of aircraft warfare against civilians, and newspapers not being allowed to comment on these events. Nair also felt that the conduct of the court martials was not satisfactory as those being tried were not permitted counsel or allowed to defend themselves. After writing to the Viceroy and failing to get justice for those whom he felt were wrongly convicted, he resigned from the Government.

Nair added that he had no ill feelings towards O'Dwyer, but felt the Lieutenant Governor was responsible for what had happened in the Punjab. He reiterated his ethical conviction that the killing of innocent men, women and children by bombs was an unjustifiable atrocity. As far as this was concerned, he noted, nobody had spoken in favour of O'Dwyer, arguing that the British in India, too, felt what was done was unjustifiable.

With regard to strikes, Nair said that they led to trouble only when officials interfered. Firing was only justifiable if the mob refused to disperse and danger to life was perceived, he argued. Aircraft should not have been used until full warning had been given and innocents had been allowed the opportunity to escape. At this point, McCardie interjected, 'Do you mean you would allow a minority to be murdered out of hand without dropping a single bomb in order to stop the massacre?'[10] Not only did the judge pose questions on behalf of the plaintiff's counsel, but he also had the privilege of interrupting the proceedings as he wished, unlike the plaintiff's counsel who would have to wait his turn to cross-examine. Nair replied that he did not think the use of bombs against women and children and in the murder of innocents was justified. Not one to

---

10 'Sir S. Nair in the Box', *The Hindu*, 30 May 1924.

relent easily, McCardie asked him whether it was a matter of ethics or practical government. Nair retorted that it was a matter of practical government because it was by use of bombs that Mesopotamia was lost to England.

As the trial proceeded, it became clear that McCardie, notwithstanding the evidence or testimonies of defence witnesses, had already arrived at the conclusion that Dyer's actions were to protect and preserve the empire and prevent anarchy, which he made clear to the jury. At regular intervals through the trial he had made it clear that he believed that Dyer's actions were correct and that O'Dwyer had been defamed. Apart from interrupting witnesses, he frequently intervened to comment on the facts and repeatedly clashed with Schwabe.

When asked about Jallianwala, Nair stated that no proper steps were taken beforehand to stop the meeting. He denied open rebellion existed in the Punjab. On cross-examination, Charles asked him if Dyer had honest reason to believe his force was in danger of being surrounded, would Nair then accede that Dyer was justified in firing at the crowd. Nair once again repeated that Dyer should have given warning for the crowds to disperse. Charles countered by asking whether an effective notice could have been given to such a crowd. Nair replied there had been ample time as Dyer had been aware of the meeting several hours earlier and Dyer could not account for his failure to prevent the meeting from being held or issuing a notice long before he arrived at the Bagh.

When Nair was asked whether he thought O'Dwyer had instigated the Punjab brutalities, he said this was for the evidence to prove. Asked whether O'Dwyer was aware of the atrocities, he said O'Dwyer must have been aware, as martial law was imposed at his request and the military was to consult him at all times.

The case had lasted for five weeks by now, of which three were devoted to depositions by the plaintiff. Thereafter, McCardie summed up the case. Despite having commented forcefully through the five weeks, McCardie spoke for seven hours over two days, while his notes filled 121 pages of the official transcript, of which 30 were on Amritsar. All of this was heard in a crowded courtroom which included the Maharajah of Kapurthala.

McCardie instructed the jury to dismiss all questions of race and colour and not be swayed by emotion. He emphasized the dangers from the Punjab's proximity to the Frontier, menaces from Afghanistan, sectional antagonisms and the paramount necessity of maintaining law and order. He also thought that aircraft could be used in extreme cases if the Government wished to repress crime and anarchy. With regard to Dyer's actions, the judge thought the word 'atrocity' should not be applied lightly to the actions of a man propelled by a sense of duty and honesty of purpose and may have been guilty only of an error in judgment. 'And the word atrocity is to be considered in connection with what I regard as the supreme duty of every government, be it in England or be it elsewhere, to maintain order and to repress an atrocity.'[11] In short, McCardie tried to argue that Dyer's actions were to maintain order and repress a

---

11 O'Dwyer, Michael, *India As I Knew It*, London: Constable & Co Ltd, 1925, p 235.

mutiny. Rhetorically, he asked what would have happened had Dyer and his force been destroyed. 'Rebellion leads to insurrection [which] leads to civil war. Civil war is a terrible thing and in the case dealing as we are with matters of high policy you have only to remember that grave evils may sometimes demand grave remedies.'[12]

McCardie charged the jury to consider the totality of the circumstances and suggested their decision must not necessarily be determined by the Hunter Committee's findings or pronouncements by the Government of India or the Secretary of State. His view was that the time and method of punishment inflicted on Dyer was most unfortunate and its severity could only be realized by those cognizant of the military sense of pride. He asked the jury to decide on O'Dwyer's direct responsibility in the events.

Despite this, McCardie said he was taken aback with regard to forced recruitments. 'The evidence is so striking, the episodes are appalling, the indecent episodes, the cruelty, the bush torture, they are appalling.'[13] At the same time, he said that some of the accounts may have been exaggerated, and may have only been isolated incidents than widespread. Justifying his statement even further, he said it was extraordinary that no complaint was made to the Government about the forced recruitments and the outrages were not mentioned in the press until long after conveniently overlooking the press censorship in Punjab at the time. On martial law, he said, 'My own view is

---

[12] O'Dwyer, Michael, *India As I Knew It*, London: Constable & Co Ltd, 1925, p 235.
[13] 'O'Dwyer–Nair Libel Suit: The Last Stage: Judge Sums Up', *The Hindu*, 4 June 1924.

that martial law, when it is once declared, should on all occasions and at all costs be administered with firmness. I think further that it should be administered with rigour because the essence of the matter is that people should know that they must obey.'[14] His concluding views were as follows:

> 'Subject to your judgement, speaking with full deliberation and knowing the whole evidence given in this case, I express my view that General Dyer in grave and exceptional circumstances acted rightly and in my opinion, upon the evidence, he was wrongly punished by the Secretary of State for India. That is my view and I need scarcely to say that I have weighed every circumstance, every new detail that was not before the Hunter Committee; but that opinion which I now express is an opinion which you as a Jury may say you disagree with and may take up another position in regard to the matter.'[15]

McCardie's conclusion left little to imagination – it was clear whose side he expected the jury to take. He asked the jury to consider two questions:
1. Whether Dyer's actions at Amritsar were an atrocity; and
2. If so, was O'Dwyer, as Lieutenant Governor of the Punjab, responsible for that atrocity?

The first question was not relevant to the case as the issue at hand was not whether or not Dyer was guilty of atrocities in the Punjab. With regard to O'Dwyer's complicity, the

---

14 O'Dwyer, Michael, *India As I Knew It*, London: Constable & Co Ltd, 1925, p 230.
15 Ibid, p 236.

judge directed the jury to disregard evidence that had been taken under deposition corroborating the facts gathered by the Hunter Committee and examined in detail by the Secretary of State for India and the Cabinet. Essentially, McCardie left no doubt as to what the jury's decision should be.

On the completion of the judge's address, counsel on both sides agreed that the questions to be put to the jury were:

1. Are the various matters presented in evidence defamatory to the plaintiff?
2. Are they true in substance and fact?
3. Are they fair comment?[16]

The jury retired at 3.05 p.m., and reconvened after nearly three hours at 5.50 p.m. Spectators rushed back into the courtroom as the jury returned. Many were surprised that a verdict had been arrived at so quickly. When everyone was seated, McCardie asked, 'Members of the jury, you have now deliberated for a long period. Have you agreed yet upon the verdict at which you should arrive?'[17]

The foreman replied, 'No, my Lord, and I do not think we ever shall.'[18]

---

16 O'Dwyer, Michael, *India As I Knew It*, London: Constable & Co Ltd, 1925, 240.
17 Ibid.
18 Ibid, p 241.

THE VERDICT

The silence was deafening. With a hung jury and an inconclusive verdict, the judge had to declare a mistrial. All eyes were now focused on McCardie, who was dumbstruck for the first time in five weeks. He had expected the jury to endorse the direction he had given and find that Sir Nair had indeed defamed O'Dwyer. This was not to be.

O'Dwyer sat glum, seemingly unable to speak. As he looked to his counsel, the grim-faced Ernest Charles, he may have wondered whether to let go or to pursue a fresh trial with another judge and yet another jury. The five weeks had taken its toll. The information regarding the atrocities inflicted in the Punjab and, in particular, the massacre at Amritsar had stunned the Empire. O'Dwyer now found that many who knew him now wished not to be associated with him. In fact, the government had asked him not to take the case to trial. Even Lord Chelmsford, now a cabinet minister, noted in his memoir that he did not endorse O'Dwyer's decision. O'Dwyer was later booed when he tried to give a speech at the Brotherhood Church in London.

Sir Nair, on the other hand, was equally surprised. Despite the clear racial bias of McCardie, his counsel had presented overwhelming evidence that O'Dwyer was indeed responsible for the Punjab atrocities. With his strong conviction in the fairness of British justice, he had believed he would be vindicated. But that was not to be.

The courtroom was abuzz. Newspaper reporters were unsure what they should do next. Should they wait to see what was going to happen or should they contact their papers and report on the verdict?

McCardie now demanded of the foreman, 'Have you considered each of the libels separately?'

The foreman confirmed, 'Yes, your honour.'

'And you are unable to arrive at a unanimous verdict?'

'Yes, my lord,' the foreman repeated.[1]

After such a long trial, McCardie did not want to declare a mistrial, nor did he want Nair to leave vindicated. As a firm believer in English superiority, he had indicated unequivocally he wanted Nair punished for the temerity of stating that a British Lieutenant Governor had committed atrocities while that officer was seeking to save the Empire from the calamity of a mutiny. McCardie then took an unprecedented step. Looking straight at the plaintiff and his counsel, he asked, 'Are you willing to take the verdict of the majority?'[2] There was a collective gasp at McCardie's unprecedented decision to choose the majority verdict. If the vote was not unanimous, a mistrial should have been declared.

---

1   O'Dwyer, Michael, *India As I Knew It*, London: Constable & Co Ltd, 1925, p 241.
2   Ibid..

Charles was taken aback. If, by some chance, the majority of the jury had voted against O'Dwyer, all would be lost. He was hesitant, though he hoped an all-English jury prodded by a supportive judge would endorse his client.

McCardie noticed the quandary he was in. He then turned to the defence and asked, 'And you, Sir Walter?'[3]

Sir Walter was not prepared to either agree or disagree. Instead, he asked for time to discuss his options. 'My lord. I would like to request a recess to confer with my client.'

McCardie had no alternative but to agree. Addressing both the defendant and the plaintiff, he announced, 'Please speak with your clients and then speak with each other and let me know. The Court will recess till 10 in the morning tomorrow.'

Nair along with his family, Schwabe and Wallington repaired to Schwabe's chambers near the Middle Temple. Schwabe felt that despite McCardie's concluding notes, the majority would favour Sir Nair as enough evidence had been presented to show that the Punjab atrocities could not have occurred without O'Dwyer's knowledge, approval and authorization. However, as a lawyer, he was aware of the damage McCardie's defence of O'Dwyer would have wreaked on the jury, and did not want to take a chance. He did not want to risk a majority vote and recommended against accepting a majority vote. Nair's son, Ramunni Menon Palat, agreed. As a barrister himself, he believed an Englishman would side with another of his kind against

---

[3] O'Dwyer, Michael, *India As I Knew It*, London: Constable & Co Ltd, 1925, p 241.

an Indian, especially when honour was at stake. Madhavan Nair, also a barrister, agreed with his brother-in-law.

Nair knew it was so. He knew first-hand of instances when Englishmen had been acquitted of an Indian's murder. However, as a judge, he believed intrinsically in the law, and that truth would prevail. He believed that the case had been adequately proven, and that no English jury would rule against him after weighing all the evidence. Having gone through intense pressure and stress for five weeks, he was tired. He looked at his wife who, though bewildered by the turn of events, smiled at him, indicating she would support him whatever he did.

The last few weeks had been trying, especially the manner in which McCardie had conducted the case. The bias apparent in his interjections, his extraordinary conclusion, and his declaration that the Secretary of State for India had wrongly censured Dyer had made a mockery of English justice. The atmosphere of prejudice was heavy. Nair had felt O'Dwyer had two counsels – Charles and McCardie. McCardie had also confounded the issue. The matter at hand was whether O'Dwyer was guilty of complicity in the atrocities, but the judge had steered the case towards the idea that O'Dwyer and Dyer were saviours of the Empire.

Nair now decided to look at the matter dispassionately. The trial was undertaken to determine whether or not O'Dwyer had indeed been responsible for the atrocities. The trial was about him. As Lieutenant Governor, O'Dwyer was the final authority on all administrative decisions made in the Punjab. He had once proudly declared that he knew at any moment what occurred in every nook and cranny in the Punjab and that nothing occurred without his approval, which is why he could forestall seditious conspiracies and anarchist plots. In the trial, however, he had claimed innocence and declared before God and man that he knew nothing of what his subordinates were doing.

Nair thought the question of whether Dyer had been rightly or wrongly condemned by the Secretary of State and the Cabinet was irrelevant to the case. The fact was that O'Dwyer had filed a case against Nair because the latter had held O'Dwyer accountable for the atrocities in his book. Yet, at the trial, it was Dyer's actions that were being discussed, heard and judged. From the very beginning McCardie had raised this issue and stated Dyer had been wrongly punished. Having no access to the Hunter report or the papers through which the Government had come to its decision, McCardie had no rationale to back his comments on Dyer's conduct. He should not have stated the massacre was necessary for the safety of the Empire, especially to an English jury in England at a time when the country was recovering from the First World War. Additionally, if the judge felt O'Dwyer had nothing to do with the massacre, there was no need to enquire whether Dyer was right or wrong. Nair concluded that McCardie was wrong in making his opinions known to the jury. This was misdirection and, on that basis alone, he felt the case should be declared a mistrial. There was also the question of whether McCardie would have behaved the same way if an eminent barrister of the calibre of Sir John Simon had represented Nair.

Nair knew that in a worst-case scenario, which was that the majority of the jury had voted against him, he could appeal. At that time, he could even represent himself. It was while they were in this dilemma that a messenger came to them from opposing counsel Ernest Charles asking whether they could discuss a matter.

Schwabe looked at Nair, who nodded and said, 'Let us hear what he has to say.'

Schwabe met Charles in his chambers, where the latter asked him what he intended to say to the judge the next day. Charles informed him that his client was not keen to go to trial again, and wanted a ruling. Schwabe agreed that a ruling would be ideal, but as the foreman had clearly stated they were unable to arrive at a unanimous verdict, he saw no alternative but to opt for a fresh trial. Charles then wondered whether Nair might agree to a majority vote should the damages be restricted to £1,000 and costs if the majority ruling went in favour of his client. The initial demand for an unconditional public apology was not mentioned. Schwabe said that he would put forth this option to his client.

When the proposal was put to Nair, his son immediately rejected it. He did not believe an English jury would vindicate his father. Nair looked questioningly at his wife. The case had taken a toll on her and she was tired. She smiled and asked Nair to decide as the law was his passion, assuring him that whatever decision he took would be the right one. Schwabe sided with Nair's son, and said that a fresh trial with a new jury would totally vindicate his position.

But Nair was tired. The case had originally been filed in the middle of 1922. Two years had passed and, during this time, the case had entirely consumed him. He wanted it to end and to get on with his life. For Nair, it had never been about the money. He had fought this case because he had been asked to give a public apology for a claim he had made in his book – a claim he believed to be true. He had refused to apologize then and instead had chosen to fight the case in an English court. Now that an apology had not been demanded, he felt vindicated. Besides, he still continued to believe in English justice and fair play. He told Schwabe to convey to Charles that he would agree to a majority ruling provided the damages were limited to £500. If, however, the ruling was in Nair's favour, he would like O'Dwyer to bear the costs plus apologize to those whom he had wronged in the Punjab, the Hunter Committee, Secretary of State Montagu, the Cabinet and the country. O'Dwyer agreed.

The stage was set. The next morning, when court resumed, McCardie asked Charles formally whether his client would accept a majority vote; Charles assented. He then turned to the counsel for the defendant. Schwabe also agreed by saying, 'Yes, my lord, I will take the verdict of the majority except on the question of damages, as to which my learned friend and I have agreed a figure if the verdict is against me.'[4]

---

4   O'Dwyer, Michael, *India As I Knew It*, London: Constable & Co Ltd, 1925, p 241.

McCardie then confirmed, 'You have both agreed to take the verdict of the majority?'[5]

Schwabe replied, 'Yes. If there is a verdict against me, that will be for the agreed amount with costs.'[6]

The judge then turned to the foreman and asked, 'Mr Foreman, you have heard the plaintiff's and defendant's decisions. Can you announce your verdict?'

The foreman said, 'My lord, a majority of 11 for the plaintiff and 1 for the defendant on all points.'[7]

The judgement was passed. Nair had been held guilty for defaming O'Dwyer. He would have to pay O'Dwyer £500 plus costs of the trial. O'Dwyer then stated that he would be willing to forgo the damages and costs if Nair tendered an apology. Nair's unequivocal rejection of the offer resounded in the courtroom. He had written only what he knew to be the truth and he firmly refused to apologize for this.

The one dissenting juror among the 12 was the Honourable Harold Laski, a reader at the London School of Economics. While his fellow jurors were probably overawed by the proceedings, persuaded by the judge's words and swayed by nationalistic feelings, Laski's reason for dissent were, 'In this summing up to the jury, Mr Justice McCardie, speaking as he said, "with full deliberation," expressed the opinion that General Dyer, who had suppressed the outbreak was unjustly condemned by the Government for the part he had played. That was a view which however important was

---

5 Ibid.
6 Ibid.
7 O'Dwyer, Michael, *India As I Knew It*, London: Constable & Co Ltd, 1925,

not strictly relevant to the case; and since the Government had refused the evidence upon which General Dyer rightly or wrongly, was condemned, he was not in possession of all the facts when he uttered his criticism of the executive. No one can doubt he acted from the highest motives but no one I think can doubt also that a judge ought not to advise a jury and through the jury the public at large upon highly controversial questions of a non-legal character upon which the jury itself has to make no findings.'[8]

Laski was absolutely correct. The jury should have arrived at their decision based on the evidence placed before them, and not as a result of the judge's prodding. Laski was the only one who had understood the case, listened to both sets of counsel, and made an informed decision.

~

Nonetheless, when Schwabe told Nair that the decision must be appealed on account of misdirection, the latter told him he accepted the verdict. Nair was now drained of all energy, exhausted by the length of the trial and by the shattering of his belief in the English justice system. Completely disillusioned by British justice, hurt and disappointed, he told Schwabe if there was another trial, who was to know if 12 other English shopkeepers would not reach the same conclusion?[9]

Schwabe asked him, 'But what about your reputation?'

---

[8] Laski, Harold, *A Grammar of Politics,* George Allen and Unwin Ltd, London, 1925, p 552.

[9] Menon, K.P.S., *C. Sankaran Nair: Builders of Modern India, Publication Division,* Ministry of Information and Broadcasting, New Delhi, 1974, p 118.

Nair quietly replied, 'If all the judges of the King's Bench together were to hold me guilty, my reputation will still not suffer.'

REVERBERATIONS

Despite the judge's bias and the odds being stacked against the defendant, the case had been a sensation in England. Newspapers in the country and in India keenly followed the proceedings, often reporting verbatim every day. Anglo-Indian and English loyalists rejoiced at hearing that O'Dwyer had been vindicated. Dyer was re-established as a hero. But, in the euphoria, the British did not notice that the crumbling of their mighty Empire had begun.

Had the trial been held in India, or heard by an impartial judge, the verdict could well have been very different. The all-English jury had shielded the men responsible for the most brutal atrocities towards a people they had subjugated. Such a decision was bound to have severe repercussions in India. The Indian people felt that they would never get justice at the hands of the English, which strengthened their will to fight for freedom. The movement for self government had received an added impetus.

The English press's reactions were mixed. Almost oblivious and unmindful of Indian sentiments, the *London Times* applauded the decision, stating that it was a powerful verdict and an assertion of the will of the English people to protect India. However, there were many who did not agree. The *Daily Chronicle* criticized McCardie, as did many prominent persons such as A.G. Gardiner, the *Nation* editor H.W. Massingham, and C.P. Scott of the *Manchester Guardian*.

The *Westminster Gazette* severely condemned McCardie's conduct during the trial, saying he had created a most disturbing precedent by criticizing the Secretary of State for India. 'If unhappy memories had to be revived the elementary sense of responsibility should have saved Justice McCardie from making statements which must have the worst effect on India. It is very remarkable that he should have committed himself to these amazing statements because General Dyer's action was not being tried and was not at issue. Anyhow it is not for a judge trying a civil case to pronounce a public absolution upon actions which have already been officially judged by the state department. No judge or jury can arrogate to themselves the functions of the Government and General Dyer's actions were public and official actions and the administration had to take or repudiate responsibility for the policy thereof.'[1]

The *Daily News* considered the case the gravest possible misfortune to the public interest of England, and expressed regretful amazement at McCardie's conduct. It argued that the judgement passed on Dyer's actions could not be reversed and that, in the minds of educated Indians, Amritsar would now be likened to the black hole of Calcutta. Similarly, with McCardie condoning acts of violence that had previously been condemned, *The Tribune* called the verdict a 'wanton misuse of judicial authority'.[2]

---

1 *Westminster Gazette*, 10 June 1924.
2 *The Tribune*, 8 June 1924.

Indian papers were even more vociferous in their reactions. *The Forward* said, 'Nowhere have we found a judge acting as counsel for the prosecution without the least pretension to ordinary decencies which lend dignity to the bench.'[3] *The Leader* said, 'The end is what everyone expected as it would be, not on the strength of the case but because of the extraordinary and unprecedented role which the learned judge deemed it fit to play in the course of the trial. The result of the case is that for Indians Sir Michael O'Dwyer is not less of an O'Dwyer than he was, whereas Sir Sankaran Nair though defeated in a Court of law has distinctly gained in stature as an independent and patriotic Indian.'[4] *The New Statesman* strongly criticized McCardie's handling of the case, which had tarnished the name of British justice and asked for him to be taken to task for the same.

McCardie's conduct led to heated discussions in the House of Commons and a motion was tabled for his removal from the bench. Suggesting that by expressing his opinion McCardie had exceeded judicial criticism, Member of Parliament George Lansbury gave notice that he would seek to put an address to the throne to have McCardie removed from the bench on the grounds that he was unfit to carry out the judicial duties attached to his high office.[5] However, Prime Minister Ramsay MacDonald thought McCardie's actions did not amount to such moral delinquency that would justify a prayer to

---

3   *The Forward*, 8 June 1924.
4   *The Leader*, 7 June 1924.
5   Nair, C. Sankaran, *Autobiography of C. Sankaran Nair*, Chennai: Lady Madhavan Nair, 1966, p 286

the King to have him removed from office. He described the findings as an *obiter dictum* (an incidental remark said in passing, or an unnecessary remark) unconcerned with the main purpose of the trial. MacDonald ascribed McCardie's vocal outburst to his lack of knowledge of the situation and to the fact that he had made the objectionable statements at the conclusion of a long, impassioned and vehement trial. He dismissed McCardie's comments as irrelevant and unfortunate but did not deem his comments as a misuse of his judicial powers. Haldane, the Chancellor, agreed with the Prime Minister.

Aggrieved at having his opinions evaluated in a derogatory light, McCardie, in turn, threatened to resign. He tried in vain to get the support of the Lord Chancellor to make a statement that the Prime Minister's comments were wholly untrue. The Secretary of State for India, Lord Olivier, sent a despatch to the Viceroy Lord Reading in Delhi, supporting the Prime Minister's rebuke of McCardie. He also derided his insolence towards Montagu and the Cabinet. On 27 August, the Prime Minister's rebuke was sent to the press. Five days later, the Viceroy expressed his agreement with Lord Olivier's criticism, but he felt that further discussions on the question were not conducive to public interest.[6]

But in defeat, there was victory. The case had garnered attention from the highest echelons of power in the British government. The *O'Dwyer v. Nair* case had informed the

---

6   Menon, K.P.S., *C. Sankaran Nair: Builders of Modern India*, Publication Division, Ministry of Information and Broadcasting, New Delhi, 1974, p 120; Colvin, Ian, The Life of General Dyer, London: William Blackwood & Sons Ltd., 1929, p 315

global press about the brutalities in Punjab. The whole world was finally made aware of the Jallianwala Bagh massacre and was horrified at the atrocities perpetuated in the Punjab. Nair, by fighting the case in an English court, had ensured that there would never again be another Jallianwala.

The people of Punjab, who had wholeheartedly supported Sir Nair, were dejected at the verdict but hailed him as a hero. Even today, there is a plaque honouring Sir Nair for his support in the museum at Jallianwala Bagh, just outside the Golden Temple. However, Sir Nair was saddened that the Congress, of which he had been a past president, did not send him a single note of encouragement or sympathy.

In the end, this was a battle Nair fought alone. He had fought for what he knew to be right, even though in the end it proved to be a lost battle.

GREY SKIES

Leaving the courthouse on 6 June 1924 was difficult for Nair. There were scores of reporters and cameramen, waiting to catch a glimpse of the actors in this controversial case. He took a deep breath before stepping out of the giant doors with which he was now familiar. He wondered how he and his family could best avoid the press. Just as they were about to step out, a jubilant O'Dwyer strode out and, almost instantly, all the reporters rushed towards him while the photographers jostled for space for their tripods and equipment. A much relieved Nair held his hand out to his wife and they left the courthouse with their heads held high, knowing that in the end, win or lose, they had lived by their principles.

The skies were dark that day, and the rain clouds had burst into a light drizzle. The weather had been unusually cold and wet through the five weeks of the trial, with very little sunshine. Yet, unmindful of the rain, the Nair couple decided to walk back to their residence. They walked in silence, with the rest of the family trailing at a short distance.

The trial had taken its toll on the sexagenarian – not so much physically as mentally. Being a man of the law and believing in the integrity of the legal process, it had been disheartening to see McCardie influencing the jury to undermine the defence. His faith in the British judicial system was shaken, and it saddened him to watch the blatant abuse of the law in court. Yet, the loss of the case and the penalties were inconsequential. He had no regrets, nor was he disappointed at losing, because he knew the case had served its purpose. He was glad the horrors of Jallianwala Bagh had now spread far and wide, and never could such a dastardly action repeat itself.

The days following the trial were relatively quiet. There were the occasional press intrusions and well-wishers who would drop in to commiserate at his loss but, for the most part, Nair returned to his regular routine of early morning yoga sessions and quiet hours in the library. However, his thoughts would frequently return to the trial. Now that he had had time to mull over matters, Nair had a change of heart and wanted to appeal against the verdict on grounds of misdirection by a partisan judge.

Accepting defeat is never easy, and when the defeat comes via unfair means, it becomes even more irksome to accept. It began to occur to Nair that maybe he had made a mistake by engaging outside counsel. He was a lawyer of the highest standing with a formidable reputation. Perhaps he should not have handed over the reins of such an important case to a counsel who was chosen at the last minute and not known for his expertise in the courtroom or of the caliber and reputation of Sir John Simon, Nair's original choice for counsel. Nair felt he could argue the case himself in the court of appeal. He seemed to be looking for any reason, beside an unfair justice system, to account for his loss. He desperately needed to restore his faith in the English justice system. After all, he was one of the very few Indians who believed that an Indian could receive an impartial hearing and a fair trial in an English court. His family dissuaded him from taking the case any further. Unlike him, they did not believe he would ever get justice in an English court, especially one presided over by an English judge.

THEREAFTER

The English court had declared its verdict. Nair paid his fine, O'Dwyer felt vindicated. McCardie moved on to a new trial but, as it turns out, the protagonists of this embroilment were to feel the impact of this trial long after it was over.

The case was meant to address O'Dwyer's action in relation to the Punjab including the Jallianwala Bagh massacre, but much of the debate had instead centred around Dyer's conduct, making the army man an integral part of the trial. Dyer's health had already begun to deteriorate before the trial, and he had excused himself from attending it on account of his poor health. Although chastised by the British Government and by Churchill, then Secretary of State for War, he still had his fair share of admirers. The *Morning Post* opened a fund for Dyer and money poured in in generous amounts from across the British Empire. Among the notable contributors was Rudyard Kipling, Poet Laureate of India, who contributed £10[1] and a note stating that he thought Dyer had done his duty as he saw fit. When the fundraising closed, the collection stood at £26,317, a princely sum

---

1   M. Troubalay, David, *Mahatma Gandhi's Satyagraha and Non Violence*, CUNY College at Staten Island, p 134; Illahi, Shereen Fatima, *Empire of Violence - Strategies of British Rule in India and Ireland in the Aftermath of the Great War*, Austin, USA: University of Texas at Austin, 2008, pp 152-153

in those days. The funds would have certainly made his transition to retired life easier.

Dyer and his wife retired to a secluded life at Somerset. However, though he was known as Brigadier General Dyer, he had only been given the rank of Brigadier General temporarily. When he lost command of the Fifth Brigade, he lost his rank too and reverted to being a colonel. He requested the War Office to permit him to keep his honorary rank but this was denied. He remained a colonel for the rest of his life.

His forced retirement had left him a broken man who was plagued with doubts about his actions at Jallianwala Bagh.[2] He was tormented by chronic illness for the rest of his life after being diagnosed with arteriosclerosis, for which the only cure was rest. Even the slightest excitement could induce a heart attack. His wife had hoped that moving to the rural county of Somerset and living a quiet life would help alleviate his suffering. Unfortunately, this was not to be. Before his death in 1927, he suffered several strokes that left him paralysed and unable to speak. It is reported that he was tormented by his inability to determine whether or not his actions at Amritsar had been right until his last. He died in the hope that he would get an answer when he met his Maker. According to Nigel Collett in *The Butcher of Amritsar: General Reginald Dyer*, Dyer reportedly said, 'So many people who knew the condition of Amritsar say I did right…but so many others say I did wrong. I only want

---

2   Ghosh, Swagata, 'The Last days of Reginald Dyer', *Sunday Chronicle*, 10 April 2016.

to die and know from my Maker whether I did right or wrong.'

~

McCardie was a maverick who practiced what today might be termed as judicial innovation. He was of the belief that the law must keep up with the times. His interpretations of the law would not necessarily comply with precedents but would be malleable to what he felt was the need of the hour. It is perhaps this manner of thinking that had him come to the *O'Dwyer v. Nair* trial with pre-conceived ideas. He had made no bones about voicing his opinions even though they weren't accurate interpretations of the facts.

However, unknown to most, the honourable judge was addicted to both women and gambling[3], according to a biography by Antony Lentin. He ended up a lonely man, unable to recover from crippling debt and hounded by creditors. Falling into deep depression, he committed suicide in 1933.

McCardie had been a favourite of the popular press during his heyday but following his retirement, he had been largely forgotten. All that remains today in memory of the judge is an unnamed bronze head on a marble stand in the Queen's Room at Middle Temple Hall.[4]

---

3 Lentin, Antony, *Mr. Justice Mc Cardie (1869–1935): Rebel, Reformer and Rogue Judge*, Cambridge: Cambridge Scholars Publishing, November 2016, p 149
4 Ibid.

Ironically and providentially, Sir Nair's portrait is prominently displayed at the National Portrait Gallery in London.

~

After winning the case, O'Dwyer maintained that Dyer and he had been vindicated in a British court. He felt he had managed to regain his reputation that had taken a beating following the Hunter Commission. In his jubilation, O'Dwyer may have hoped that he would now be free of the scars of the unsavoury episode. But that was not meant to be.

His endorsement of General Dyer's massacre at Jallianwala Bagh would come back to haunt him. On 13 March 1940, Udham Singh, a washerman in Amritsar who had been wounded in the massacre and had seen thousands shot dead and wounded, fired two bullets at O'Dwyer in Caxton Hall in London, killing him instantly. After killing him, Udham Singh made no attempt to escape arrest. At his trial, standing tall and proud, he showed no remorse for his actions. Instead, he boldly informed the court that he had killed O'Dwyer because O'Dwyer had wanted to kill the spirit of his people, the people of the Punjab. This was Udham Singh's way of getting payback against Britain and its people for his countrymen who were still suffering humiliation, torture and starvation under British rule. Udham Singh believed there could be no greater honour for him than to die defending his people and his motherland.

~

Nair, on the other hand, returned to India a few months after the case had concluded. He decided to continue his fight for justice for the people of India and was elected overwhelmingly to the Council of State from the Landholder's Constituency in Malabar. His reforms included the creation of a self-governing Tamil Province consisting of 10 districts in the Madras Presidency. Another of his proposals was that no further political progress should be undertaken in India until the system of communal electorates was abolished – the intent being to get Hindus and Muslims together. The tensions and conflicts between the two communities were a cause for deep unhappiness and regret for Sir Nair until his last breath.

Both Nair and his wife were theists and towards the latter years of his life, he turned even more towards religion. In April 1926, the two went on a pilgrimage to Badrinath. Located about 10,800 feet above sea level, one had to hike through a difficult trail to get there. As they neared the shrine, they saw a holy man of striking appearance coming down a hill. As he approached them, Lady Nair got down from her palanquin and respectfully touched his feet. She asked him when she would meet the Lord. The holy man said, 'Soon.' They reached the temple that night, and after prayers, were housed within its premises. The next morning, when Nair tried to wake his wife, she did not stir – she had passed away during the night. This was a terrible blow for Nair, who was left devastated. He dearly missed her companionship and support. She had been a pillar of strength, taking on the responsibilities of the home and upbringing of their six children – five daughters and one son – on her own, allowing him to focus on his career.

Nair returned to Delhi to continue as an independent member of the Council of State. In 1928, a royal commission, headed by Sir John Simon, was formed to look into the workings of the Montagu-Chelmsford reforms and to consider what other steps needed to be taken to advance self-government in India. It was decided that, along with the commission composed entirely of Englishmen, there must be an Indian Central Committee of six. Nair was offered the chairmanship of this committee. His belief was that Indians should formulate the scheme of self-government and not Englishmen. Under Nair's direction, the commission asked for a clear declaration by the English Parliament that India will get full dominion status and that this would be done without any further commissions being appointed. Before the commission's report was published, the Viceroy promised dominion status for India within the British Empire. With this, Nair felt he had completed his mission and decided to retire from public life.

He spent the last summer of his life with his daughter and son-in-law in Sri Lanka (then Ceylon). At 76, he was active and fit. In March 1934, his third son-in-law, M.A. Candeth, passed away suddenly. On hearing of his death, Nair rushed with his son to be by his daughter's side. While travelling, his car met with an accident. Nair suffered a head injury, from which he never recovered. A month later, on 24 April 1934, at his eldest daughter Lady Madhavan Nair's home, Nair breathed his last as family priests chanted Vedic hymns in an adjoining room.

~

The site of the terrible massacre has stood, since that fateful day of 13 April 1919, as a silent reminder of the many innocent lives lost to imperial violence. A trust was founded in 1920 to build a memorial at the Jallianwala Bagh site and the plot was purchased. Inside the public garden, an independent India built a memorial in 1951 in the memory of those who had died in the massacre. A flame was added in remembrance as a tribute to the martyrs. Within the museum, along with pictures of some of the martyrs, are the portraits of Udham Singh and Sir Sankaran Nair, a befitting acknowledgement of his contribution to the fight against injustice and brutality in the Punjab.

Dignitaries from around the world have visited the compound since then and have offered their regrets and respects, including Queen Elizabeth II in 1997, who described the massacre as a 'distressing example of moments of sadness in Anglo-Indian History'.[5] In February 2013, the then British Prime Minister David Cameron laid a wreath at the memorial and described the massacre as 'a deeply shameful event in British History, one that Winston Churchill described as monstrous. We must never forget what happened here and must ensure that the UK stands for peaceful protests.'[6] Sadly, he did not deem it necessary to apologize to the Indian people. His successor, Theresa May, also repeated his sentiments but her words fell short of an outright apology.

---

5   *Book of Condolences* at Jallianwala Museum.
6   Ibid.

AFTERWORD

An Indian taking on an Englishman in an English court, presided over by an English judge and before an entirely English jury, seemed destined for failure from the start. Adding to this was the fact that most of the defendants' witnesses were, being Indian, unable to be present in court to testify. But Nair's unshakable faith in the integrity of the law, no matter where it was practiced, saw him take on his opponent single-handedly. His faith in British justice was so strong that when the jury was unable to decide on a unanimous verdict and even when his lawyers advised him not to assent to a majority decision, Nair failed to see that a court of law could be biased against him.

Despite the defeat, Nair achieved his primary goal which was to expose the injustices and cruelties the British had meted out to the people of the Punjab. The Punjab atrocities could no longer be confined to the lanes of Amritsar. The trial had brought them to the notice of the entire world. This was an era when the written word – newspapers – were the main source for global information. A trial in England between an Indian and an Englishman, already a rare occurrence in those days, attracted a lot of attention. The courts were filled to capacity and the press covered the trial daily. Soon, every gory detail of the brutalities that were hitherto confined to the provincial borders of the Punjab became common knowledge to anyone who picked up a newspaper in India or elsewhere in the British Empire.

In India, the case had the people doubting the credibility of the English justice system. In the Punjab, reports of the trial caused grave damage to Sikh loyalty to England. Their resolve to avenge their dead strengthened. Reports of the rejoicing of the English and Anglo Indian community at the victory of O'Dwyer only added salt to the wounds of a people already devastated by abuse and massacre. From being a simple matter of defamation, the case had turned into a trial of a regime.

The verdict transformed those who had been fairly moderate in their opinions towards the Empire. The people of India were now convinced that Gandhi was quite right to conclude that Indians were unlikely to receive fair and just treatment from an English government. The verdict ensured the civil disobedience movement received a boost and India's resolve to gain independence became even more resolute.

The case had put the British government on trial and their efforts to establish an amenable transition of power to Indians became decidedly more difficult. Press reports in India now made it apparent to the British that the people were no longer in the mood for conciliation. Consequently, the Simon Commission set up to review the Government of India Act was met with utmost suspicion, boycotted and rejected outright as it comprised seven Englishman and not a single Indian.[1]

---

1 Menon, K.M.P., 'The Ethics of Defying the Invincible: The Memorable Case of O'Dwyer vs Nair', *Asian Journal of Professional Ethics and Management*, Bengaluru, January–March 2010, p 125

Following this debacle, an Indian Central Committee of six Indians was constituted under the chairmanship of Sir Nair, its objective being that Indians, not Englishmen, should decide the blueprint for self-government.

The *O'Dwyer v. Nair* libel trial ended in a victory for the Englishman, but its lateral impact of exposing British excesses and the rise in Indian nationalistic sentiments was sufficient vindication for Nair. His primary focus had always been to do what he considered right and to ensure justice above all. His trial contributed to exposing British representatives' abuse of power and propelled the independence movement. Above all, it ensured his primary objective which was, as he says in his autobiography, that, 'There would be no more Jallianwala Baghs in India.'[2]

This was echoed by none other than Mahatma Gandhi. Commenting on the *O'Dwyer v. Nair* case judgment, Gandhi wrote in *Young India* on 12 June 1924, 'A most intimate Jewish friend often used the expression "Rabbi May" to signify that the highest in the land may commit the most atrocious crimes not only with impunity, but may even carry with them popular congratulations for those crimes. The expression may be fittingly useful in connection with the *O'Dwyer v. Nair* case. The judge showed bias from the very commencement. Day after day, the report of the case was painful reading for the public and though the judgment was a foregone conclusion, the public had hoped against hope that the judge will do some measure of justice in his summing up and judgment. It was not to be. The worst has happened. But a British judge may do

---

[2] Nair, C. Sankaran, *Autobiography of C. Sankaran Nair*, Madras: Lady Madhavan Nair, 1966, p 125

with impunity what an Indian may have to lose his head over. By accepting Sir Michael O'Dwyer's challenge Sir Sankaran Nair has put the British constitution and the British people on trial. They have been tried and found wanting. Even in this simple matter, a man of Sir Sankaran Nair's proved loyalty could not get justice. If Sir M. O'Dwyer had lost, all the British Empire would not have gone to pieces, but its false prestige would have suffered a bit and were not the British people pledged to stand by their faithful servants even though they might at times make mistakes, so long as they were in favour of the Empire which enriched them. I know that Sir Sankaran Nair has the sympathy of every Indian in his defeat. For me it was a foregone conclusion. As the case dragged along its weary length I admired Sir Sankaran Nair's pluck in fighting a forlorn cause. He has provided one more powerful count in the indictment against the present rule which must be ended at any cost.'[3]

It would be another 25 years before India got independence, but the reverberations of the case continued to influence public opinion through this period. The Jallianwala Bagh massacre had shown the world the excesses of the British Empire, and it convinced the Indians that they could not receive justice in a country ruled by foreigners. The resultant protests directed at and the boycott of the Simon Commission proved this, while the Civil Disobedience Movement also received a fillip. The moderates of the past disappeared; no Indian trusted the British anymore. It would be this feeling that would guide the independence movement from then on.

In defeat, Nair had won a greater victory.

---

[3] *Young India*, 12 June 1924

BIBLIOGRAPHY

'Chelmsford in the Box', *The Hindu*, 7 May 1924.

'Indian Press Comments', *The Hindu*, 7 June 1924.

'Jallianwala Bagh Massacre: Remember General Dyer. Here are the dying words of the Butcher of Amritsar', *Financial Express*, 13 April 2018.

'Jeffries Come to Judgement', *The Hindu*, 6 June 1924.

'London Letter: Deputations at work – Mr. Sastri's Statements', *The Hindu*, 30 May 1924.

'Mahatmaji's Comments: Another Indictment of the Present System', *The Hindu*, 12 June 1924.

'More Evidence: Recruiting Scandals', *The Hindu*, 24 May 1924.

'O'Dwyer Nair Libel Suit: Frank Johnson in the Box – Martial Law Days', *The Hindu*, 15 May 1924.

'O'Dwyer–Nair Case: More Evidence – Lala Harkishen Lal', *The Hindu*, 27 May 1924.

'O'Dwyer–Nair Libel Suit: Flogging Incidents – Powers of Government', *The Hindu*, 6 May 1924.

'O'Dwyer–Nair Libel Suit: Gen Dyer's Deeds – Moral Effect Theory', *The Hindu,* 5 May 1924.

'O'Dwyer–Nair Libel Suit: More Evidence – Recruiting Methods', *The Hindu,* 3 May 1924.

'O'Dwyer–Nair Libel Suit: Progress of Trial – General Sir W. Beynon', *The Hindu,* 13 May 1924.

'O'Dwyer–Nair Libel Suit: The Final Stages – Sir W. Schwabe's Address', *The Hindu,* 2 June 1924.

'O'Dwyer–Nair Libel Suit: The Last Stage: Judge Sums Up', *The Hindu,* 4 June 1924.

'Plaintiff wins £500 and costs', *The Hindu,* 5 June 1924.

'Press Comments: Liberal Criticism', *The Hindu,* 7 June 1924.

'Sir S. Nair in the Box', *The Hindu,* 29 May 1924.

'The Defence Case: Counsel's Arguments', *The Hindu,* 21 May 1924.

'The O'Dwyer Case–A Detailed Report: The opening scenes – Plaintiff's Counsel's Address', *The Hindu,* 1 May 1924.

'The O'Dwyer- Nair Case', *The Strait Times,* 27 September 1924.

The Premier on the McCardie Case', *The Hindu,* 26 June 1924.

'Thrown to the Wolves', *The Strait Times,* 4 June 1924.

'Vindicates General in Amritsar Affair', Kingston, Jamaica: *Gleaner (The) Newspaper*, 14 June 1926.

'Young India: Another indictment of the present system 19-06-1924', Ahmedabad: *The Hindu*, 1924.

Agrarian Condition of Punjab, Shodhganga infibnet.pdf (last accessed on 3 October 2018).

Allaboutsikhs.com, sikhee.com/ Maharajah and Sikhiwiki (last accessed on 4 October 2018).

Associated Press of India, 'Pandit Jagat named as witness', *The Hindu*, 9 May 1924.

Bannerjee, Himadri, *Agrarian Society of the Punjab, 1849-1901*, Manohar Publishers and Distributors, New Delhi: 1 August 1983.

Collett, Nigel A., *Journal of the Royal Asiatic Society*, Third Series, Vol. 21 Part 4, October 2011.

Collett, Nigel A., *The Jallianawalla Bagh Revisited – I*, New Delhi: United Service Institution of India.

Collett, Nigel A., *The Jallianawalla Bagh Revisited – II*, New Delhi: United Service Institution of India.

Collett, Nigel A., *The O'Dwyer v. Nair Libel Case of 1924: New Evidence Concerning Indian Attitudes and British Intelligence During the 1919 Punjab Disturbance,* London: Royal Asiatic Society, 2011.

Collett, Nigel, 'A muse abused: The Politicizing of the Amritsar Massacre', *Review of Nick Lloyd's Book on the Amritsar Massacre: Our Tribes*, 17 July 2012.

Collett, Nigel, *The Butcher of Amritsar: Brigader General Reginald Dyer,* London: Hambledon Continuum, 2006.

Colvin, Ian, *The Life of General Dyer,* London: William Blackwood & Sons Ltd., 1929.

CWMG Project of Government of India, 1956.

D'Shea Joe, 'Murder, Mutiny & Mayhem – The blackest villains from Irish History', O'Brien Press, 2012.

Darling, Sir Malcolm, *The Punjab Peasant: In prosperity and debt,* Oxford, UK: Oxford University Press, 1928.

Disorders Inquiry Committee, *The Hunter Report,* Superintendent Government Printing, Calcutta, India: 1919-1920.

Furneax, Rupert, *Massacre at Amritsar,* London: George Allen Unwin Ltd., 1963.

Gandhi, Mahatma, 'Congress Report on the Punjab Disorders', *The Collected Works of Mahatma Gandhi,* Vol. 20: 25 March 1920–June 1920.

Ghosh, Swagata, 'The Last Days of General Dyer', *Sunday Chronicle,* 10 April 2016.

Griffin, Sir Lepel Henry, *Ranjit Singh,* Oxford, UK: Clarendon Press, 1908.

His Honour Sir Michael O' Dwyer GCIE: KCSI Lieutenant Governor of the Punjab, London: Forgotten Books, FB & C Ltd, 2018.

Illahi, Shereen Fatima, *Empire of Violence - Strategies of British Rule in India and Ireland in the Aftermath of the Great War*, Austin, USA: University of Texas at Austin, 2008.

Irish, Major MSC Bell R., 'Massacre at Amritsar: The origins of the British approach of minimal force on public order operations', Kansas: School of Advanced Military Studies, 2009.

Kaul, Chandrika, *Reporting the Raj: The British Press and India,* Manchester: University Press, 2003.

Lal, Vinay, 'The Incident of the "Crawling Lane" – Women in the Punjab Disturbances of 1919', *Genders* No. 16, Texas: University of Texas Press, 1993.

Laski, Harold, *A Grammar of Politics*, George Allen and Unwin Ltd, London, 1925

Lentin, Antony, *Mr. Justice Mc Cardie (1869–1935): Rebel, Reformer and Rogue Judge*, Cambridge: Cambridge Scholars Publishing, November 2016.

Malaviya, Kapil Deva, *Punjab: Open Rebellion in the Punjab with Special Reference to Amritsar*, Los Angeles, California: Hard Press Publishing, 1 August 2012.

Menon, K.M.P., 'The Ethics of Defying the Invincible: The Memorable Case of O'Dwyer vs Nair', *Asian Journal of Professional Ethics and Management,* Bengaluru, January–March 2010.

Menon, K.P.S, *Many Worlds:* An Autobiography, Mumbai: Oxford University Press, 1965.

Menon, K.P.S., *C. Sankaran Nair: Builders of Modern India,* Publication Division, Ministry of Information and Broadcasting, New Delhi, 1974.

Mittal, S.C., *Freedom Movement in India 1905–29,* New Delhi, Concept Publishing Company, 1977.

Montagu Papers, British Library, MSS EUR D 523, 523/8.

Montagu, Edwin S., *An Indian Diary,* London: William Heinemann Ltd., 1930.

Muthiah, S., 'Taking on British Justice', *The Hindu,* 30 April 2018.

Nair, C. Sankaran, *Autobiography of C. Sankaran Nair,* Madras: Lady Madhavan Nair, 1966.

Nair, C. Sankaran, *Gandhi and Anarchy,* Madras: Tagore & Company, 1922

Nair, C. Sankaran, S. Rajasekaran Nair (ed.), *Autobiography of C. Sankaran Nair,* Ottapalam, Kerala: Chettur Sankaran Nair Foundation, 1998.

Nair, Sir C. Madhavan, *A Short Life of Sir C. Sankaran Nair: Builders of Modern India,* Publication Division, Ministry of Information and Broadcasting, 1967.

National Archives of India, *Home, Political,* No. 377, February 1920.

O'Dwyer, Michael, *India As I Knew It,* London: Constable & Co Ltd, 1925.

Papers of 1st Viscount Chelmsford as Viceroy of India 1916-1921, London: The British Library, Asian and African Studies, 1916-1921.

Pathak, Rashmi, *Punjab through the Ages*, New Delhi: Sarup & Sons, 2007.

Reed, Stanley, *The India I Knew, 1897–1947*, Watford, UK: Oldhams Press, 1952.

Reuters Agency, 'O'Dwyer–Nair Libel Suit: Progress of Trial – More evidence', *The Hindu*, 8 May 1924.

Reuters Agency, 'O'Dwyer–Nair Suit: More Evidence – Captain Batting', *The Hindu*, 20 May 1924.

Reuters Agency, 'O'Dwyer–Sir Nair Libel Suit – Hearing opening the plaintiffs case', *The Hindu*, 30 April 1924.

Reuters Agency, 'The Defence Case', *The Hindu*, 23 May 1924.

Reuters Agency, 'The O'Dwyer Case: Questions in Commons – Enquiry Called For', *The Hindu*, 16 June 1924.

Saha, Abhishek, 'I had to fire well. Jallianwala Bagh butcher General Dyer's testimony', *Hindustan Times*, 15 April 2015.

Talbot, Ian A., *The Punjab Under Colonialism: Order and Transformation in British India*, Southampton: University of Southampton, January 2011.

Talbot, Strobe, *Engaging India: Diplomacy, Democracy and the Bomb*, Washington DC, USA: Brookings Institution, March 2006.

The Imperial Recruitment Policy, http://shodhganga.inflibnet.ac.in/bitstream/10603/172252/9/09_chaper%202.pdf (last accessed on 4 October 2018).

Traboulay, David M., 'Mahatma Gandhi's Satyagraha & Non-violent Resistance – Fall 1997', CUNY Academic Works, 1997.

Wolpert, Stanley, *An Error of Judgment*, Boston: Little Brown Company, 1970.

Woodruff, Philip, *The Men Who Ruled India: The Guardians*, Jarrold & Sons, Norwich, United Kingdom 1963.

Yadav, K.C., *Donning the Khaki: Recruitment in the Punjab during the First World War*, New Delhi: United Services Institution of India.

Yadav, Y.C., *Centennial Remembrance: Recruiting Terrorism during World War 1: A Case Study of Punjab*, New Delhi: USI, 30 October 2016.

ACKNOWLEDGEMENTS

This book has been a first for us in many ways. Both of us have been writing for several years but we write on entirely different subjects; this is the first time we have collaborated to write a book. It is also our first venture into the historical non-fiction segment.

For years, we have been writing books commissioned by publishers or books on subjects that had been enthusiastically supported by publishers prior to our actually writing them. This was the first time, however, that we wrote a book without the backing of a publisher. We were delighted, therefore, when Bloomsbury India decided to take on the book.

Working with Bloomsbury has been very pleasant and our many interactions have been cordial and easy. We must, of course, make special mention of Prerna Vohra, who was always readily available to us over the phone and email. Prerna promptly answered our many queries and it has been a pleasure working with her. We would like to acknowledge and thank Bloomsbury and Prerna for their unstinting support and help.

Finding our publisher would not have been possible if it had not been for our literary agent Anish Chandy. Finding a literary agent for our publication was also a first and we were fortunate that Anish from his very first reading of our first draft, which was more of a synopsis of the book, decided to back us and encouraged, supported and advised us each step of the way. His faith in the subject matter of the book and in us had us enthused and eager to get on with the project and complete it in record time.

It would be remiss if we did not thank Justice Chettur Sankaran Nair – a worthy namesake of Sir Sankaran Nair – an eminent lawyer and judge in his own right and a grand nephew of Sir Nair. We approached him to write the foreword to this book and the octogenarian agreed with great enthusiasm. He read the manuscript and wrote the foreword in a matter of ten days, despite not being in the best of health at that time. Not just that, he also went through the chapters in great detail and gave us information that enriched the book. He was generous with his time and we cannot thank him enough for all his help and encouragement.

Our sincere and heartfelt thanks go to Justice Thottathil B. Radhakrishnan, Chief Justice of the High Court of Calcutta. Despite his busy schedule, Justice Radhakrishnan readily agreed to give us his valued comments. When we approached him, he was quick to respond and his words are of great value to us.

Finally, we would like to thank our immediate family who spurred us on to write this book. Our daughters, Divya and Nikhila, and their incredibly supportive husbands, Aditya Hitkari and Vivan Bhathena, who have always been generous with their ideas, suggestions and have even often brought to our attention aspects we might have otherwise overlooked.

We believe that Sir C. Sankaran Nair's story was one that needed to be told. Here was a man who rose to the highest echelons of power in the government but who thought nothing of giving up his position and power when he believed the government he represented had denied his countrymen justice and had committed atrocities under the guise of keeping law and order. This was the man who made Indians realize that they could not expect justice at the hands of an English government and who hastened India's march to Independence.

We have enjoyed writing this book and, in its writing, we have learnt so much about an ancestor who contributed significantly to India achieving Independence – someone who was strong but fair, fearless and principled; a man worthy of emulation.